THE SPIRITUAL DYNAMICES OF
EFFECTIVE LEADERSHIP

A Simple Goide to Sharing Your Faith with Confidence and Cultural Awareness

GLEN E. KERR

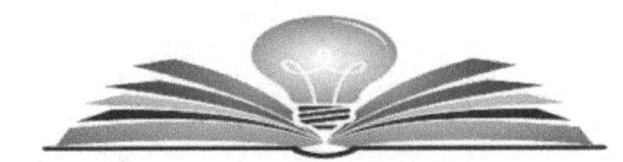

WORD OF KNOWLEDGE
PUBLISHING

WHERE CURIOUS MINDS ARE ILLUMINATED

Copyright © 2015 by Apostle/Pastor Glen E Kerr

ISBN 978-971-959-69-12

The author asserts his moral right to be identified as the author of this work.

All Rights reserved solely by the author. No part of this publication may be reproduced, copied, stored in a retrieval system, or transmitted, in any form or by any means, without the prior written consent of the copyright holder, nor be otherwise circulated in any form of binding or cover other than that in which it is published and without a similar condition being imposed on the subsequent purchaser.

Unless otherwise indicated, Bible quotations are taken from the New King James version of the Bible. Copyright © 2002 by Thomas Nelson.

Published by Word of Knowledge Publishing

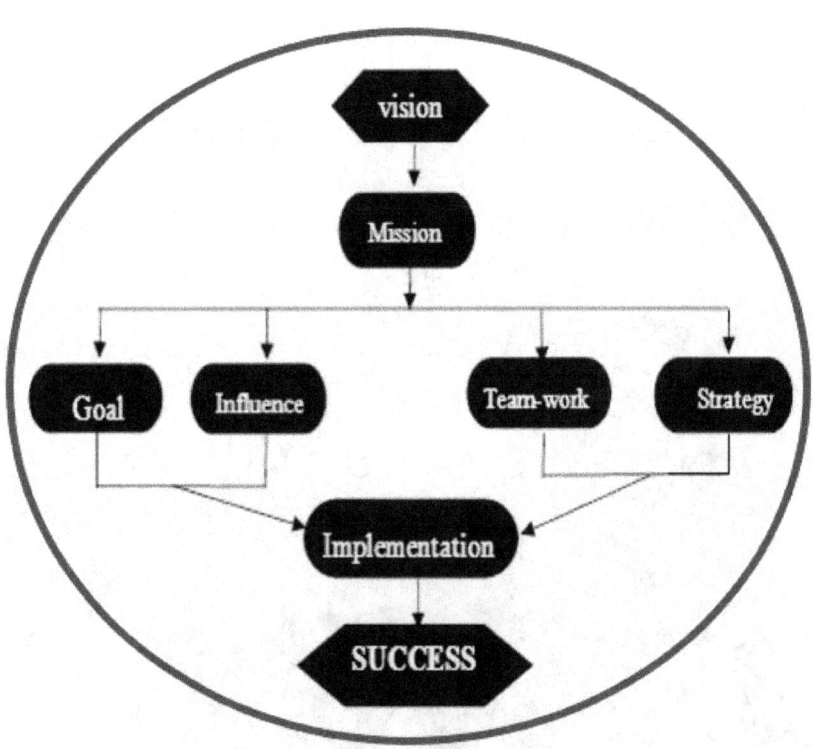

ONE OF THE GOLDEN RULES OF SUCCESS

OR TAKING THAT FIRST STEP

CONTENTS

Dedication	IX
Acknowledgement	XI
Introduction MAXIMISING YOUR LEADERSHIP EFFECTIVENESS	XIII
SECTION ONE INCREASING YOUR CAPACITY TO EXCEL	XXI
A GREAT LEADER IS A DELIVERER OF THESE ATTRIBUTES	XXII
1. Unlocking Your Full Leadership Potential	1
2. Increasing Your Capacity To Excel	19
3. Successful Spiritual Leaders Are Not Smarter Than You	41
4. The Maturity Process	77
SECTION TWO HOW TO RAISE SUCCESSFUL LEADERS	95

5. Raising Leaders (A Human Perspective) — 97

6. God's Pattern for Raising Leaders — 113

SECTION THREE — 137
BIBLICAL MODELS OF

TO MAKE IT TO THE TOP; — 138

7. Old Testament Model of Leadership — 139

8. New Testament Model of Leadership — 161
   Jesus—A New Testament Model

SECTION FOUR — 173
HOW TO INCREASE YOUR PROSPECT OF SUCCESS WITH IMMEDIATE EFFECT

HOW TO GAIN TRUE LEADERSHIP — 174

9. How to Increase Your Prospect of Success With Immediate Effect — 175

10. Making it Happen/Some Protocols — 203

11. Summary and Basic Rules Not to Ignore — 223
    Basic Rules of Leadership

Bibliography — 229

Autobiography — 232

Other Books by the Author   233
How to Effectively Share Your Faith With Confidence,
Compassion and Understanding, Regardless of a Persons
Background in Easy Steps

A Study Guide to Personal Evangelism   234

Embracing Your Challenges   235
How Courage, Confidence, and Faith Transform Hardship
Into Triumph and Success

DEDICATION

This book is lovingly dedicated to the cherished memory of my late Uncle and Pastor, Reverend Ezra A. Kerr. He possessed an extraordinary blend of intelligence and humility, navigating life with a spirit of integrity that inspired those around him. His unwavering faith and godly character were evident in every interaction, and his exceptional leadership skills guided many through their spiritual journeys.

I am profoundly grateful for the invaluable spiritual guidance and support you provided throughout my life. Your presence left an indelible mark, not just on me but on the lives of countless individuals who were fortunate enough to know you. Your legacy of love, wisdom, and compassion continues to be deeply admired, respected, and emulated by all who strive to follow in your footsteps.

To my parents—you are my heroes, the pillars of strength in my life, and I love you more than words can express.

To all believers in Christ, especially those who have committed themselves to the noble pursuit of "seeking first the Kingdom of God and His righteousness...", may your paths be filled with grace and purpose.

ACKNOWLEDGEMENT

First, I would like to honor the Holy Spirit, who inspired me to write this book. I give Him all the glory, honor, and praise.

Sincere gratitude to my parents Mr. Joscelyn and Mrs. Greta Kerr, this book is a direct result of your labor of love, prayers, counsel and encouragement through the years. I want you to know that I am eternally appreciative of your love and faithfulness in the service of the Lord. The pre-eminence of your love, support and particularly your prayers cannot be overstated. God bless you always.

To my wonderful wife Jennifer, thank you, hon. Your support, encouragement, and understanding have been invaluable during this writing process. I love you very much.

I cannot overlook the incredible support of those who worked alongside me on this project, especially my proofreaders: Akin Oyediran, Nnadozie Ogwueleka, Pastor Noel Wilson, and Pastor Sam O. Adewunmi, the author of *Good Finish to Bad Start*. Your contributions have been invaluable, and I pray that God abundantly blesses each of you.

I would like to extend my heartfelt gratitude to all my dedicated partners at Pneuma Life Transformation Ministries International. Words cannot fully express my deep appreciation for your support, especially during challenging times. I pray that in due season, you will receive a reward that is "exceedingly abundantly above all that you can ask or think, according to the power that works in you."

I am deeply grateful to my mentors, colleagues, and leaders worldwide (USA, Canada, Europe, Asia, Africa, and the Caribbean); your counsel and encouragement have been poignant in helping me find my purpose and shape my destiny.

INTRODUCTION

MAXIMISING YOUR LEADERSHIP EFFECTIVENESS

Have you ever wondered why people called by God, trained in all aspects of leadership, anointed and appointed often fail to fulfill their God-ordained destiny and purpose, achieve maximum impact, and experience great rewards of success?

Statistics confirm the inconceivable reality that in the United States alone, 7,000 churches close each year, 1,700 pastors leave the ministry each month, and 90% of pastors feel they are not adequately trained to meet ministry demands.

Sunscape Ministries of Colorado, an organization serving "Clergy in Crisis," reported that more than 1,600 ministers are forced to resign from their pulpits or have their jobs terminated each month. And to make matters worse, many denominations report an "empty pulpit crisis," where they cannot find ministers to fill positions. This is a tragedy and has been the case since time began. Jesus echoed this sentiment in **Mathew 9:37**: "The harvest truly is plentiful, but laborers are few." This means laborers are in short supply because very few are available. The good news is that the book you are holding and reading provides your first critical step toward avoiding these statistics.

Whether you are a parent, a corporate executive, or a minister, you are a leader—just as God ordained you to be. And if God has ordained you to lead, you should have no fear, doubts, or inhibition when assuming your leadership responsibility because your success is guaranteed. The issue is that, as the statistics above suggest, this is not always how things unfold in practice. Ironically, simply accepting your leadership position does not guarantee success. Not even the best theological seminary can prepare you for the real-life challenges of leadership, so if you aspire to become a successful leader, this book is tailored for you. Inside, you will discover everything you need to achieve success. You will find policies for accessing your treasure trove of heavenly wisdom to fulfill the destiny God has ordained for your life and ministry. This text outlines principles for unlocking your full leadership potential, maximizing your impact, and enhancing your capacity for excellence. It describes how God empowers ordinary individuals—just like you—to achieve great accomplishments, even if they possess little or no academic qualifications, theological knowledge, or personal accolades. In this book, you will learn how aspiring leaders can effectively guide their teams, cultivate a positive and productive environment, and achieve lasting success by developing the attributes, skills, and values discussed.

I have been privileged to travel to several countries worldwide, speaking in churches, schools, and Bible colleges, as well as to leaders and leadership organizations. In the process, I have met and interacted with a range of people, including bishops, pastors, evangelists, youth workers, church custodians, and students. These people come from diverse backgrounds, cultures, religious traditions, educational levels, and levels of spiritual maturity.

Having labored for many years in the accountancy and management professions, I also met and interacted with people from the political and corporate worlds. Among them were some highly successful businesspeople; many excelled in their personal, spiritual, academic, and professional lives and ministries. That, however, is the good news. The bad news is that many leaders I encountered, together with their organizations, paint a bleak image of hopelessness and despair. Their struggles paint a vivid picture of challenges that weighed heavily on their ambitions and aspirations. Again, if this resonates with you, there is no need to worry; help is available. Embracing the spiritual Dynamics of effective leadership is all you need.

My extensive knowledge, experience, and research have given me insights into why leaders succeed or fail. I aim to share these insights in this book to help you avoid similar pitfalls.

It is quite disheartening to walk into a church or any other organization and see clearly on display why a ministry or organization may not succeed. Very often, the evidence greets you at the door. For example, a few years ago, I was invited to a church for the first time, and upon arrival, the first person I met was the usher, who asked me, "how can I help you?" I was astounded by this approach and asked myself, "Am I in church or a candy store?" Some of you may consider this to be trivial, but the usher should have extended a warm, welcoming right hand, with a smiling face and a word of welcome, such as Nice to have you today, please take a seat, and I hope you will enjoy the service. Believe it or not "first impressions last." Some ministries and other organizations have been struggling for years, and although the evidence is clear, their leaders either cannot see it or have seen it but have no idea how to resolve the problem.

Whatever the reason, this is a poor representation of the powerful organization Christ founded on earth and, indeed, of what Peter and a few others experienced on the Day of Pentecost (**Acts 2**). Some churches are in the early stages of development. Still, it's clear that no suitable building blocks are in place to foster growth and development for the foreseeable future. In addition, some leaders appear to have no noticeable vision; even if they do, no one in the organization knows it. Worse still are those who do not seem to have a personal relationship with God or a godly passion for the work. They have no aims, objectives, or sense of purpose. This is like someone who boards a bus or train without knowing where it is going. And of course, as Lewis Caroll (English Logician, Mathematician, and Novelist, primarily remembered for Alice's Adventures in Wonderland) once said, ''If you don't know where you are going, any road will get you there'' This is to say, how can you pick the right road when you do not know where you are going; you can't say one route is better than the other. You are bound to end up anywhere and with disastrous consequences. For the leader, this is inevitable failure.

In the following chapters, we will discuss this and other reasons leaders fail, together with answers that address them. In the process, I want to help you become the influential and successful leader God called and anointed you to be. This will be accomplished by providing basic step-by-step options to help you achieve your goals.

The aim of this book is not to load you down with more theoretical information on leadership when, in fact, there are already a plethora of books available on the subject. Instead, this is a simple and practical guide to help you address issues you are likely to encounter daily.

Following at least 40% of the principles in this book will add new and improved values to your leadership skills, giving you a cutting edge among leaders. You will stand head and shoulders above your peers and take you to new dimensions that will ultimately bring you success.

The objective is to help you plan your journey while avoiding detrimental stumbling blocks. More importantly, it is to help you get it right the first time so you do not have to return to correct mistakes that could have been avoided. This can be time-consuming and costly.

This will also provide you with a comprehensive analysis of the role of spiritual leadership and how to lead effectively. For those who are followers or not yet assigned a leadership role, this is designed to help you understand how you are being led and to give you the tools and ability to lay a solid foundation for success. And for those already in position, the wisdom and knowledge you will gain here will inevitably help you function more expertly and efficiently.

In contrast, you are destined to fail if you cannot use resources and take strategic advantage when resolute proactive leadership is essential. "Leaders who cannot deliver on their promises will not be successful. Leadership is about performance—therefore, intentions must align with results for leaders to be effective." Addressing these issues will restore balance to the Body of Christ.

To address these issues, you will need a basic understanding of spiritual leadership and the essential requirements to unlock your full leadership potential. The spiritual dynamics of effective spiritual leadership encompass knowledge and skills across several disciplines. For example, it addresses whether successful leaders are born or made. I might as well tell you now that I believe that, as in any other field, some are indeed born gifted, but by the time you finish reading this book, you will come to the conclusion that successful leaders are made; those born gifted are only given a head start.

You should also develop a practical understanding of what will bring you success and equip yourself with the tools needed to get the job done for God's glory. For example, you will understand why successful leaders are not more innovative than you are, how to increase your capacity to excel, and how to make an impact on your followers. It will help you understand why and how successful leaders choose and develop other leaders, how to create an atmosphere for growth, and how to follow God's divine order for leaders.

Many leaders fail to realize their full potential simply because they pay little or no attention to advancing their leadership skills. Most need help finding the time to rummage through the abundance of leadership information available. Others lack the proper academic background and believe they cannot succeed, even if they try. Some lack appropriate training and exposure to effective leadership policies and principles and, as a result, feel a sense of hopelessness and inadequacy. Whether you hold a position of leadership or you are just aspiring to become one, the leadership principles taught in this book will provide you with a good foundation for success.

It does not make any difference who you are—a highly trained bible scholar, a bible college undergraduate, a seasoned professional, a business manager, a pastor, or a housewife and mother. Your background does not matter. If you have doubts about achieving success, don't despair because help is at hand.

The instructions, guidance, and principles in this book come to you through observation, divine revelation, and the inspired word of God. This is to say that this is how God intended it to be, demonstrated it to be, and said it should be, as inspired by lessons taught in the Scriptures.

> This is why ordinary people like you can become successful leaders.

Section 1 outlines key steps to develop your skills. This shows you how to unlock your full leadership potential, increase your capacity to excel, and help you understand why successful leaders are not smarter than you.

Section 2 tells you how leaders are raised, as demonstrated by God.

Section 3 guides you through a couple of Old and New Testament models of leadership and

Section 4 provides insights on how to increase your chances of success with immediate effects.

Not Only for People in Ministry

Let me reiterate that while the material in this book will significantly benefit those already in leadership, it will also benefit those preparing for what God has called them to accomplish. Those who have yet to assume a leadership position but want to understand the fundamental principles of leadership will find this a great resource. For these and other reasons, I have dedicated a whole section to emphasizing "how" leaders get into their leadership positions—an area I believe is vital yet often overlooked.

Finally, anointed and successful leadership is grounded in sound doctrine and divine revelation. For this reason, we will embark on a journey beyond mere theoretical theology, delving deep into the heart and mind of God, the ultimate Author of our faith. As we seek to understand His intentions for biblical leadership, you'll gain comprehensive, coherent insight into your role as a leader through His eyes. By embracing and applying these principles, you will experience a revolutionary shift in your mindset, unlock your full potential, and elevate your skills to unprecedented heights. This transformative process will enhance your effectiveness and empower you to lead purposefully and confidently, aligned with God's vision. **Welcome to the journey.**

SECTION ONE

INCREASING YOUR CAPACITY TO EXCEL

CHAPTERS 1 – 4

A GREAT LEADER IS A DELIVERER OF THESE ATTRIBUTES

Chapter One
UNLOCKING YOUR FULL LEADERSHIP POTENTIAL

Becoming a spiritually dynamic, successful leader may seem daunting, but it's far more attainable than you might think. If you're ready to unlock your unrealized potential, **"The Spiritual Dynamics of Effective Leadership"** is your ultimate guide to achieving maximum effectiveness and becoming an influential, successful leader. This book isn't just for those who already see themselves as leaders—it's for anyone seeking to discover the path to authentic leadership. The resources included in this book will provide you with insights that will help you gain perspective to see and understand:

- **The journey through which successful leaders are forged, and**
- **How to discern if you're being led in the right direction.**

Before we dive into the principles that underpin successful leadership, let me ask you this: Have you ever wondered why some people reach the top while others, despite their best efforts, fall short? Why do individuals without formal credentials often emerge as some of the most effective leaders? What secrets do they possess that set them apart?

These questions are at the heart of our exploration. In this chapter, we'll highlight key insights to guide effective leadership and equip you with the tools to embark on this transformative journey. To do this, let's clarify some of the misconceptions you may have embraced over time.

For church leaders and church-goers alike, effective leadership is often the subject of considerable debate about the best approach. It can also be the subject of much disagreement and conflict. This often leads to divisions that spell doom for the local church and other organizations. Some priceless long-term relationships are torn apart and even cause some people to give up on their faith in God, mistakenly believing He is responsible. Most importantly, this situation is enough to render any organizational leadership ineffective and powerless.

Disagreements and conflicts are not the only reasons church leadership may be rendered ineffective and powerless. It is important to understand that holding a leadership position doesn't necessarily mean someone has met the role's requirements. For example, they may not have been raised according to God's pattern; in other words, not all leaders are of the same standard.

The challenges confronting many organizations and followers today are recognition and discernment. Followers cannot distinguish good leaders from bad ones, and organizations cannot identify candidates most suitable for leadership positions. They often choose people for the wrong reasons, a leading cause of poor effectiveness and performance.

I know no one is perfect, but given the importance of a leader's responsibility, leaders who consistently fail cannot be considered adequate and, even worse, cannot even be regarded as leaders, no matter how much you wish they were. While past accomplishments are not always a conclusive indicator of future results, a long-term track record of failure should always be addressed.

In addition, a spiritually dynamic leader must always understand, appreciate, and embrace the concept of devotion to performing their duties above themselves. In other words, serving others should always take precedence over self-serving. By serving others first, you will generate the trust, confidence, and loyalty of those you lead. This is important because leaders are only influential if their team is enthusiastic about following them. On the other hand, if a leader receives a vote of no confidence, they have essentially failed.

Successful spiritual leaders are adaptable, led by the Spirit of the Lord, and must necessitate the gifts and input of others. A clergy-driven modus operandi (method of operation), is not compatible with spiritual leadership in the 21st Century. A collective approach is preferable. Consequently, you must listen, get involved, and learn from the people you lead. Everyone has an opinion, and very often, irrespective of how insignificant it may appear to be, people's thoughts, ideas, and suggestions can significantly benefit you who are in charge. Understanding the importance of adaptive leadership is crucial in today's fast-paced and ever-changing world. Here are several compelling reasons why this topic should matter to you:

1. **Survival in Challenging Environments**: Unexpected challenges arise regularly in churches as well as industries ranging from technolo-

gy to healthcare. Leaders who adapt swiftly are more likely to navigate crises effectively, ensuring their organizations survive and thrive. For instance, companies that adapted during the COVID-19 pandemic, such as distilleries that started producing hand sanitizer, demonstrated the importance of flexibility in maintaining relevance and ensuring business continuity.

2. **Enhanced Decision-Making**: Leaders who can assess situations and adjust their strategies accordingly are better equipped to make informed decisions. By embracing flexibility, they gather diverse perspectives, leading to creative solutions that can outperform larger, rigidly structured organizations.

3. **Fostering a Resilient Culture**: When leaders exemplify adaptability, they inspire their teams to embrace change rather than fear it. A culture that values resilience encourages innovation and problem-solving, leading to increased followers' morale and innovativeness. For instance, companies like Google promote a culture of experimentation in which teams are encouraged to take risks, leading to groundbreaking products such as Gmail.

4. **Long-Term Success and Growth**: Organizations with adaptive leaders are often more sustainable over time. These leaders can best anticipate change and their followers' needs, enabling their organizations to evolve and advance. In today's fast-paced world, adapting to new trends and technological advancements is crucial for any organization, including those with a spiritual mission. Take a note from Grace Network, a Christian organization that successfully transitioned from traditional, in-person ministry to a dynamic, digital platform.

Grace Network originally relied heavily on physical church gatherings, community events, and printed materials to spread its message and connect with its community. However, as societal habits changed and digital consumption increased, they faced the challenge of remaining relevant and accessible to a broader audience.

Just as Netflix transitioned from DVD rentals to streaming services, Grace Network embraced digital transformation. They launched an interactive online platform, offering live-streamed worship services, virtual Bible study groups, and an extensive library of digital resources, including e-books, podcasts, and video series.

Grace Network's digital transformation enabled it to stay ahead of the curve, reach a global audience, and remain an essential spiritual resource for thousands. By adapting their model to meet the demands of a digital age, they not only preserved their mission but expanded it, demonstrating the power of innovation and adaptability.

5. **Personal Development**: Adapting to change isn't just about organizational success; it also enriches personal growth. Leaders who cultivate these skills become more confident and versatile, positioning themselves for career advancement. Whether it's through embracing new technology or enhancing interpersonal skills, those who adapt are often seen as assets in any workplace.

In summary, recognizing and responding to changing circumstances is not just a skill for leaders; it's an essential ingredient for success in any endeavor. By embracing this mindset, you can optimize your potential and move closer to achieving your dreams.

1.0 Understanding what it is not

Gaining a deep understanding of the spiritual dynamics of effective leadership is crucial for achieving true success. This awareness helps you recognize the qualities that contribute to strong leadership and highlights the pitfalls and misconceptions that can hinder your journey. By exploring these dimensions, you can cultivate a more meaningful and impactful leadership style that resonates with others and fosters growth. To achieve this, it is important to understand what it is not.

1.1 It is Not Your Title or Position

To become a successful leader, the first and most important concept to understand is that leadership is not about your title or position. We live in a time when titles and positions often seem to define everything. People everywhere are defined by their titles rather than by their abilities, character, or integrity. And although we expect such things in the secular world, it has no place in the Kingdom of God. This is not my idea; it is without doubt pertinent to the teachings of God's Holy Scriptures, as I will explain later. This notion of title and position has strained the Body of Christ for generations and is one of the greatest hindrances to successful spiritual leadership.

As an example, in the community where I grew up, a skilled tradesman such as a tailor would quickly become known as a *"tailor." (Taylor)* Or someone might introduce another as Mr. So-and-So, the accountant. You might have even heard someone say, "Do you know who I am?" referring to their position in the community or church. The problem is that people often fail to live up to their titles or positions. This is a far more significant issue within the Body of Christ than you may realize. Many hold positions and have titles, but have very little else to show for it. Unfortunately, some would not even move a muscle without titles. Their only passion is high-ranking positions or elevated chairs from which to look down on others.

This reminds me of a few years ago when I was on a leadership training course. The leader who taught the lessons shared a real-life example of this. A local church held a meeting to appoint people to leadership positions. One of the appointees, who had previously served as a deacon, was now appointed to a ministerial position. At the end of the meeting, the leader asked (let's say his name was Deacon Brown) "Deacon Brown, can you please close us off in prayer?" However, Deacon Brown, now known as Minister Brown, refused to pray in defiance, as if to say, "Who are you calling Deacon Brown? Or, I am not Deacon Brown; I am Minister Brown."

On another occasion, I shared my thoughts with a friend about people becoming caught up in titles and positions. She began to laugh and told a similar story about attending a function at her local Church. During the lunch break, one of the bishops sat down to eat. To illustrate, let's assume the bishop's family name was Josephs, often shortened to Bishop Josephs. Another person who attended the meetings greeted him, saying, "How are you, Brother Josephs, instead of Bishop Josephs?" According to my friend, the bishop created an ugly scene; he reportedly reacted badly by asking, "Do you know who I am?" In other words, please address me using only the title "Bishop."

This behavior indicates that those who embrace position and title as a statement of their achievement are mistaken. Most people mistakenly believe leadership success is due to their titles or positions. However, I must emphasize that successful leadership has nothing to do with titles or positions. Your name does not have to be a household word for God to use you to accomplish great things for His kingdom. God seldom chooses the best-looking, most robust, or most charismatic to execute His plan and purpose. In reality, this is one of those areas where God's ideal starkly contrasts with human beings. In a later chapter, I expand on this in greater detail when discussing God's criteria for raising leaders.

1.2 It is Not Your Possessions

As with title and position, the Body of Christ is also guilty of being misled by the lure of affluence. Some use money to influence others to give them leadership positions. Others will only offer their services in exchange for cash. Scripture refers to such people as hirelings. According to the International Standard Bible Encyclopedia (1915), the word "hireling" occurs only in John 11:12, where the neglect of the sheep is contrasted unfavorably with the care and courage of the shepherd who owns them, leads them to pastures, and lays down his life for their protection from danger and death. On the other hand, hirelings do their job only for money and show no love, care, or loyalty to the people, and would never give their lives for the sheep.

Not only that, but many leaders appoint people to leadership positions simply because they are wealthy or connected and can attract the affluent. The objective is to meet massive budgets, often leading to compromising the truth. Ultimately, it's easy to see how this practice can change God's divine plan to fulfill man's selfish desire. Of course, this is a trap of the enemy designed to derail God's plan and ultimately prevent you from reaping success.

1.3 It is Not Earthly Wisdom

Even those with multiple degrees listed behind their names are not necessarily God's choice for leadership positions. And what do you think is the reason for this? The answer is it takes much more than academic success to move in the fullness of the Holy Spirit. Again, this is not to say you should not seek to acquire the highest educational qualifications. In fact, I would urge you to get a PhD if you so desire. All I am saying is that your PHD or your MA in divinity does not <u>necessarily</u> qualify you for spiritual leadership. In God's Kingdom, achievement does not come from earthly credentials. Notice that Jesus started His ministry with twelve seemingly unimportant people. Having said this, these twelve people were far more significant than you can imagine. In biblical numerology, the number twelve means God's government of grace. Although most of these men were ordinary, uneducated people, note how successful they became once fully trained. Even before they were fully developed, Jesus appointed and sent out seventy others for on-the-job training, and it was a great success. **Luke 10:17** says, "Then the seventy returned with joy, saying, Lord, even the demons are subjected to us in your name.' " Once He finished training the twelve to be servant leaders, He sent them to the world, and on their first day of ministry following His ascension, over three thousand people believed the message about Jesus and were added to the church. **(See Acts 2:41)**. A few years later, it was said of the disciples, "These who turned the world upside down have come here too" **(Acts 17:6 NKJV)**. Therefore, no matter how unimportant you consider yourself to be, you can turn the world upside down with the proper training and development, just as these ordinary men did. The question you might want to ask here is, if it is not earthly wisdom, what is it?

1.4 The Wisdom of God

The wisdom of God is unquestionably one of the most important building blocks you require if you are going to become a successful spiritual leader. "Wisdom is the principal thing; therefore, get wisdom. Overall, you're gaining an understanding. Exalt her; she will promote you and honor you when you embrace her. She will place on your head an ornament of grace. A crown of glory she will deliver to you." **Proverbs 4:7-9.** On the surface, this may appear to be an impossible impasse, but you will be delighted to know that acquiring this kind of wisdom is very simple. James **5:1** says: "If any man lacks wisdom, let him ask of God, who gives to everyone liberally." This is, therefore, a good place to begin—ask God for wisdom on how to become an effective spiritual leader, and you can "rest assured" He will give it to you graciously. This is exactly what Solomon did, and he became the wisest man who ever lived. "Now the king went to Gibeon to sacrifice there, for that *was* the great high place: Solomon offered a thousand burnt offerings on that altar. At Gibeon, the Lord appeared to Solomon in a dream by night, and God said, "Ask! What shall I give you?" **1 Kings 3:4-5.**

What would you choose if faced with the dilemma of God offering to give you anything you desire? I believe the vast majority would probably ask for riches and honor. Nevertheless, not Solomon; he had the presence of mind and the understanding to ask for wisdom to lead the people of God. We should all do as Solomon did and seek wisdom.

> *"And Solomon said: "You have shown great mercy to Your servant David my father, because he walked before You in truth, in righteousness, and in uprightness of heart with You; You have continued this great kindness for him, and You have given him a son to sit on his throne, as it is this day. Now, O Lord my God, You have made Your servant king instead of my father David, but I am a little child; I do not know how to go out or come in. And Your servant is in the midst of Your people whom You have chosen, a great people, too numerous to be numbered or counted. Therefore, give to Your servant an understanding heart to judge Your people that I may discern between good and evil. For who is able to judge this great people of Yours?"*

Observe how God responded. He fulfilled the request and exceeded expectations. God provided him with riches, honor, and a long life, which is truly remarkable. As Jesus said, "Seek first the kingdom of God and His righteousness, and all these things shall be added to you." **Matthew 6:33**

> *"The speech pleased the Lord that Solomon had asked this thing. Then God said to him: "Because you have asked this thing, and have not asked long life for yourself, nor have asked riches for yourself, nor have asked the life of your enemies, but have asked for yourself understanding to discern*

justice, behold, I have done according to your words; see, I have given you a wise and understanding heart, so that there has not been anyone like you before you, nor shall any like you arise after you. And I have also given you what you have not asked: both riches and honor so that there shall not be anyone like you among the kings all your days. So if you walk in My ways, to keep My statutes and My commandments, as your father David walked, then I will lengthen your days." **1 Kings 3:6-14.**

Solomon was young and inexperienced, but he knew he needed to address problematic leadership decisions at the start of his reign. He understood that he needed to make wise decisions when leading the people of God. Solomon was required to resolve conflicts wisely and prioritize to obtain the best interpretation in a given situation. He needed to choose the right people for critical roles in his palace. He understood that he could not work with disloyal or rebellious people, no matter how influential they appeared. He needed to ensure his team included people committed to working in his best interest. He dealt with men hungry for titles and positions, including his brother Adonijah, who sought to establish his own kingdom. But one by one, through the wisdom God gave him, Solomon could discern the loyalty of those around him and remove all those who refused to cooperate.

Perhaps you know of leaders with several degrees behind their names who speak eloquently but are struggling to succeed in ministry. As previously mentioned, the call of God and the anointing are more important than degrees and expressive skills. Also, as previously indicated, some of the most outstanding leaders we read about in the

Bible were neither highly educated nor the most excellent speakers. These were people who encountered God and embraced his influence with passion. Even some highly educated individuals renounced their former lifestyles to become effective in the kingdom.

To emphasize this point, and as discussed in greater detail in a later chapter, when God searched for a man to free the children of Israel from bondage, He turned to Moses, whose history included stammering, murdering, and taking care of sheep on the backside of the desert until he met God at the burning bush. When God looked for a king after His own heart, He chose David, the youngest, least likely among the sons of Jesse, who wasn't even invited to what was his anointing service. David was caring for sheep when God chose him above his well-trained brothers to be anointed as king over Israel. Note the connection here: taking care of sheep. Then you have people like Elijah, who found Elisha plowing a field. When God called Jeremiah, he argued that he was too young and could not speak. Jesus wasn't even acknowledged by James and Jude, His half-brothers, and someone even dared to ask whether anything good could come from Nazareth. God tends to choose those who aren't trying to impress others. He chooses ordinary people to do extraordinary things, and these are those who are likely to transform the world for Christ.

We know Moses was educated, but he was not a gifted speaker, as he admitted. From a human perspective, he certainly would not have been your first choice.

The Apostle Paul was also highly educated, trained at the feet of Gamaliel, but renounced that aspect of earthly wisdom for the excellence of knowing Christ. In his own words, he wrote,

> *"But what things were gain to me, these I have counted loss for Christ. Yet indeed I also count all things loss for the excellence of the knowledge of Christ Jesus my Lord, for whom I have suffered the loss of all things, and count them as rubbish, that I may gain Christ and be found in Him, not having my own righteousness, which is from the law, but that which is through faith in Christ, the righteousness which is from God by faith; that I may know Him and the power of His resurrection, and the fellowship of His sufferings, being conformed to His death, if by any means, I may attain to the resurrection from the dead." Philippians 3:7-11*

As strange as it may sound, to lead effectively, you are encouraged to get understanding but not to "lean on your own understanding." "Do not be wise in your own eyes; fear the Lord and depart from evil." "It will be health to your flesh and strength to your bones." **Proverbs 3:7-8.** Ungodly wisdom can pose a risk to the spiritual leader. It suggests to me then that what is needed is a mind change, i.e., godly leaders are always encouraged to think from God's perspective! The Apostle stated, "Do not be conformed to this world, but be transformed by renewing your mind" (**Romans 12:2**).

Spiritually dynamic and successful leaders have great imaginations—walking in God's wisdom carries much more weight than man's. The knowledge of God made you understand you should always put the interests of others before your own. "Let nothing be done through self-ambition or conceit, but in lowliness of mind let every man esteems each other better than himself. Let each of you look out not only for his interests but also for the interests of others" (**Philippians 2:3-4**). Successful leaders always think about better ways of doing things because they are unsatisfied with the ordinary. They desire to experience the extraordinary. Nothing gives a true leader greater satisfaction than seeing genuine transformation and growth in the lives of the people they lead. They want to see themselves and their people growing in grace, going deeper into the things of God. A godly leader thinks creatively and refuses to limit God to the ordinary.

There can be no limits or boundaries concerning God or what you set out to achieve as a leader. It should be standard for godly leaders to think of themselves as winners because they desire to see God's demonstrative power at work in their lives. But it is also imperative that godly leaders exercise a degree of autonomy; that is, when necessary, they must be able to think and make decisions without undue external pressure. There should be a real sense of awareness of what will bring success. If you are unfamiliar with engaging your discernment, you will always be off course. Taking a "stab in the dark" is no better than being led by a blind man. We all recall the scripture that says, "If the blind lead the blind, both will fall into the ditch."

Moreover, effective spiritual leaders must be able to think quickly and seek divine insight from God. Their foremost responsibility is to motivate and guide God's people toward a life of holiness, fostering spiritual maturity and encouraging a profound and intimate walk with the Lord. Through their actions and commitment, they significantly contribute to building a community that embodies the essence of God's love and divine purpose. Their efforts foster an environment filled with compassion, support, and shared values, ultimately enriching the lives of those around them.

In the upcoming chapter, we will explore strategies to significantly increase your capacity to excel. Get ready to unlock your true capabilities!

Chapter Checklist

In review:

- Why do some people with no credentials make it to the top while others fail?

- The topic of successful leadership is often a topic of a great deal of controversy.

- Successful leadership is also a subject of much disagreement and conflict, often resulting in division that spells doom for many organizations.

- It causes long-term relationships to be torn apart and even causes some to give up on their faith.

- It renders any organizational leadership powerless.

- Having a title or a position does not necessarily mean you are a leader.

- There can be no limits or boundaries regarding what you can achieve as a leader.

- You must understand that leadership is not your position, not about your possession, and not earthly wisdom, but successful leaders must pursue godly wisdom.

Personal Notes

Chapter Two
INCREASING YOUR CAPACITY TO EXCEL

Every individual has the capacity to expand their potential and attain a level of excellence that transcends their current thinking. This principle is especially pertinent in the realm of leadership. Each spiritual leader, regardless of their current level of development, has the inherent potential for growth and skill development. Acknowledging and embracing this opportunity can help achieve greater results and have a more significant impact on one's leadership endeavors.

The fundamental reason behind this lies in the fact that every spiritual leader is inherently equipped with a unique ability to profoundly transform the lives of those they encounter. Within you resides the potential to attain the highest level of achievement, as envisioned by God. While it is the calling of leaders to act as catalysts for revolutionary change in their followers' lives, not everyone experiences the profound impact such leadership can bring. To become a spiritually dynamic and successful 21st-century leader, you will need to know how to increase your capacity to excel in your position of authority. Increasing your capacity to excel will enable you to execute tasks with greater precision. Ultimately, your success hinges on your ability to solve problems effectively, and your ability to resolve problems equals success. This means successful spiritual leaders are great problem solvers by choice and inspiration. Therefore, if you want to excel, you must understand and appreciate the challenges leaders face today and how to rise to them.

To further emphasize this point, an effective leader must embrace a positive mindset when confronting intricate challenges. This approach involves not only a strong sense of faith and unwavering determination but also a deep-rooted spiritual stability. By fostering an optimistic perspective, leaders can inspire confidence in their teams, navigate uncertainty with resilience, and cultivate an environment where creative solutions can flourish.

God has not only called you to be a leader, but He has also called you to achieve greatness. The question is, why do so many spiritual leaders struggle to achieve true success? A recent article published in the "American Psychologist" suggested that leaders are not bad people but that the modern work culture sets them up to fail. Therefore, if you want to avoid failure, you must understand why leaders fail and develop effective strategies to address them.

Statistics show that many individuals enroll in theological seminaries and other educational institutions each year to acquire the knowledge and skills needed to become successful leaders. However, when the "rubber meets the road," and they face the harsh reality of real people with real problems, many suddenly realize that it takes much more than theology to address these issues. People are desperate for leaders to help them overcome their challenges in the trenches. For example, people need help with sickness, sadness, grief, worry, and pain. They need prayers, earnest demon-busting prayers. They are seeking leaders who will be there in times of need. This implies that the spiritual leader faces the important challenge of harmonizing religious doctrine with the immediate, practical assistance required by those in their community. For instance, they must provide guidance and support to a single parent who is working tirelessly to make ends meet while also caring for their children. At the same time, the leader should offer compassion and help to an elderly widow who may feel isolated and in need of companionship and resources. Balancing these roles is crucial to fostering a nurturing and supportive environment for all individuals seeking assistance. As you may have discovered by now, it is essential to minister compassionately as Jesus did. However, it is also essential that you aim to create an excellent first impression. This will help you avoid becoming overwhelmed by the endless array of problems that may arise.

In the following paragraphs, we will discuss some of the main reasons leaders fail and offer suggestions for avoiding those pitfalls.

2.1 Unrealistic Expectation

One of the main factors that causes leaders, especially spiritual leaders, to fail is unrealistic expectations by the people they lead. It is no secret that spiritual leaders are presumed to possess divinely super-spiritual abilities. The people you lead will often demand to see every vital attribute of a leader in you—including administrative skills, decision-making ability, ability to delegate, creativity, intuition, ability to inspire, and decisiveness, to name a few. However, while a leader may possess one or more of these qualities, it is implausible for any person to encapsulate all the vital qualities of a leader.

Followers are often disappointed when they discover you are only another imperfect human. However, you must avoid getting caught up in the mindset that you must prove you embody this capability. This would only prove you are trying to become a "pleaser of men," which will undoubtedly lead to disaster for you and your followers in the long run. Your attitude must be sincere and humble if you are going to make it to the top. Despite what the people you lead may think, you must lead with honesty and integrity, so please do not be pressured to prove you have superhuman abilities, because you do not.

2.2 Lack of self-confidence

Many leaders fail due to low self-esteem stemming from their physical appearance, educational background, economic or social status, or how they are perceived by others. Whatever the reason, you cannot afford to be insecure. In the first place, insecurity is a recipe for disaster when it comes to leadership. Furthermore, "God has not given us a spirit of fear, but of power and love and a sound mind" (**2 Timothy 1:7**). None of these external pressures or challenges should undermine your effectiveness as a leader. Instead, you should draw strength and reassurance from the profound love of God, the transformative power He instills within you, and the guiding presence of the Holy Spirit. This deep-rooted sense of security cultivates a steadfast maturity in you, immune to manipulation or influence from others or circumstances. Embrace this foundation, allowing it to empower your leadership and guide your decisions with confidence and grace.

2.3 Selfish Ambition and Materialism

Make no mistake: one of the most significant contributors to the downfall of leaders is selfish ambition and materialism. This is one of the tools the enemy effectively uses to divert spiritual leaders from their destiny and purpose. It is often cunningly disguised under what has become known as the "prosperity doctrine." Everyone is doing it, so why shouldn't I? Besides, I deserve it. I am a great man/woman of God. Look at the great work I am doing. So God has blessed you, and instead of blessing others, you set yourself up as a superstar living larger than life, having no regard for even that poor widow in your congregation. Frankly, this mindset is outrageous, entirely out of place in the Body of Christ, and must be urgently addressed. You should only be greedy for the 'Rhema' word of God. "But Jesus answered him, saying. It is written: man shall not live by bread alone, but by every word of God" **Luke 4:4.** Remember, love is the fulfillment of God's law, and love is not something you say; it's what you do, ''and now abides faith, hope, charity, these three, but the greatest of these is charity'' (**1 Corinthians 13:13**). Please do not let it be said that selfishness and greed have been your downfall.

2.4 Failure to include others in the decision-making process

Failure to involve others in decision-making is another cause of leadership failure. That is, "I am in control, and my decision is final." Research by the **University of Kent and Colleagues** states: "A large part of the problem with many modern organizations is their hierarchies. Leaders are at the top of the chain and are assumed to have all the answers, so they make most of the decisions." In this sense, spiritual organizations are not exempt. The reality is that knowledge and expertise are evenly distributed among people in any organization, though this fact is rarely acknowledged. The real problem is that leaders often feel too insecure to allow others to use their gifts. Unfortunately, while others may have incredible gifts and insights to address problems, leaders often feel they must be seen leading.

This demands that they act in ways that may lead them to make unwise choices and even to fail to consult the Holy Spirit for answers. The fact is that leaders do not necessarily make better decisions than their followers, and sometimes they do things that are counterproductive.

The study mentioned above pointed out that "it is better to agree that leaders are not always the best people to make the decisions. Delegating responsibilities and incorporating more inclusive approaches to decision-making can yield significantly better results."

This collaborative method not only enhances the team's overall effectiveness but also alleviates some of the burdens leaders typically carry. As leaders share decision-making, team members feel more engaged and valued, fostering a greater sense of appreciation for the journey they undertake together. Consequently, this collective effort and involvement lead to a more enjoyable and rewarding experience for everyone involved.

2.5 Loneliness at the Top

You may have heard the old dictum, "It's lonely at the top." This is often true, as being in a leadership position can indeed feel quite isolating. If you have experience in leading people, you may have already encountered this loneliness. What do you think are some of the reasons for this feeling? Here are a few suggestions to consider.

2.6 Misinterpretation of Actual Intention

The first suggestion offers an opportunity to clarify a possible misinterpretation of genuine intentions. The fundamental issue is that people in positions of authority tend to believe that the kindness they receive from followers and others comes with hidden agendas or ulterior motives. In this scenario, misinterpretation of others' intentions separates leaders from followers and prevents them from trusting each other's motives. The reason for this is simple. A person in authority may tend to see others as opportunists who use kind words and hospitable deeds for their gains. For such reasons, leaders may question the generosity and integrity of the people they lead. A leader's mindset regarding the motivation behind people's actions can ultimately drive them to disconnect from others and become isolated, with devastating consequences.

2.7 Mistrust

As it is with misinterpretation of actual intention, some leaders can be apprehensive about trusting others. Some even believe there is "no such thing as loyalty". Years ago, I used to hear a high-flying city of London Stock Exchange workers saying their dog was their only friend. Put another way, they do not wish to invite humans into their world for obvious reasons. As a leader, you must not hold such a view.

You have heard the old saying: "No man is an island; no man stands alone." This is probably more relevant where leadership is concerned. You can't do it all alone, no matter how gifted you may consider yourself to be. **Wikipedia** explains distrust (or mistrust) as "A formal way of not any one too much in a situation of grave or deep . It is commonly expressed in as a division or balance of powers, or in politics to validate terms." Corporate governance relies on distrust: the board does not trust the reports it receives from management but is empowered to investigate and challenge them. The fact that they rarely investigate or make any such challenges in most organizations, including churches, is a sign that the relationship has broken down. In secular organizations, the result is ''a'' and calls for . In the Body of Christ, leadership scandals and church splits are inevitable.

As previously mentioned, if you do not learn to utilize the gift and support of others, you could end up on your own. This will make you an easy candidate for isolation at the top. Remember, ''a three-fold card is not easily broken.' Irrespective of your opinion, trust is the driving force behind every effective relationship. When you trust someone, you understand that the person will act in your best interest, even when you are not monitoring them. Trust can hugely benefit interpersonal relationships in the Body of Christ, as in other organizations. Not only because it feels better to work with people you trust but also because it reduces the time and effort it takes to resolve problems. For that reason, you must understand that the people you lead face significant disadvantages and are not prioritizing their own agendas. You can trust their methods of operation and communication; there's no reason to be suspicious. You can be assured that they are working in your best interest. What you need to be mindful of here, though, is that trust doesn't happen automatically; it has to be developed. Some effective methods of developing trust are exchanging small gestures, showing and accepting kindness, etc. Accordingly, for leaders to build meaningful relationships, one of the most productive ways is building trust.

2.8 Lack of Devotion and Respect

Another reason power can isolate a leader is a lack of devotion and respect. In my early years, I worked for a commercial bank in the vibrant city of Kingston, Jamaica. During my time there, I observed that my employers followed a 'promote and transfer' policy. This meant that every promotion came with a transfer, either moving an employee from one department to another or from one branch to the next. I believe this was meant to prevent a colleague from becoming resentful, particularly when promoted and non-promoted individuals are at the same level in the organization. In some cases, the employee who was not promoted may have been with the company for much longer and could even have played a role in the training and development of the employee who was promoted. This situation can lead to a lack of respect for the new boss, which may reduce the non-promoted colleague's commitment, especially regarding their interpersonal relationships.

Consequently, power can significantly damage relationships. Surprisingly, this might be the best opportunity to develop your relationship into something special and advance your career and skills. The promotion of your colleague could be the route through which you could gain your promotion, and you could be their means of avoiding isolation at the top. This is much like the Joseph-and-the-butler scenario in **Genesis 40 and 41.** That relationship was vital in getting Joseph out of prison and into his position of authority. Putting the will of God aside for a moment. If Joseph had been resentful and bitter, he probably would have lost the opportunity to move into his place of power and authority. In other words, never forget to celebrate people's success. Your time will come, and others will celebrate you when it does.

Research indicates that individuals in positions of power frequently exhibit skepticism toward others' intentions. As a result, those who interact with authority figures are often perceived as having dubious motives. However, this viewpoint does not necessarily align with the actual motivations of these individuals, despite the impressions held by those in power.

In a study conducted by M. Ena Inesi of London Business School and Adam D. Galinsky of the Kellogg Graduate School of Management at Northwestern University, participants were asked to evaluate either a peer or a subordinate who had either done them a favor or simply completed their required tasks. The findings revealed that participants trusted their subordinates less than their equally powered peers, but only after receiving a favor; trust did not decrease after the completion of necessary work. These results mean that those in power do not necessarily feel suspicious of their colleagues every day. Instead, it is in the moment that someone tries to establish closeness through generous acts and unrequested favors that mistrust gets in the way. Overall, mistrust weaves a 'cynical psychological web' in that the powerful see only selfishness and refuse to respond positively when it comes to favors. Accordingly, this strangles trust and ultimately results in less enthusiasm. These psychological and social processes can leave the mighty lonely at the top, so what can you do?

- You should never be too hasty to draw a negative conclusion in these circumstances. Try to regain your composure and discern the motivation behind your kindness.

- Consider the person's behavioral patterns and character traits. For example, is this someone who is genuinely courteous, or is this someone who ordinarily does things for favors?

- You must engage your spirit of discernment and try to see beyond the surface. This will give you a greater advantage in distinguishing between a show of kindness and dishonesty.

It is important to note that favors motivated by self-centered intentions are not necessarily bad. While you may still want to exercise caution and avoid leaving yourself exposed, resolve in your heart to be grateful by saying "thank you." Showing your appreciation in such small ways can create a more positive spiritual environment. Adapting these simple but fundamental principles will go a long way in preventing the powerful from being isolated at the top.

2.9 Pride and Arrogance

A superiority complex is one of the most significant stumbling blocks that cause a leader to fail. The superiority complex is characterized by pride, arrogance, and self-importance. Leaders can become the center of attention in this context. Impressed with themselves and their achievements, they take credit for God's gift, believing the world revolves around them. Such thinking causes leaders to think they are better than others and that the rules no longer apply. This often leaves little room for submission to God and compassion for others. This is certainly not the right direction for any godly leader, yet many have been down this road. Success in itself can be a pitfall in this regard. Many of those whose ministries grew quickly and beyond their expectations have fallen for the devil's greatest trick to capture the heart of a successful man and draw him away from God, his first love, so that he loves only himself. The rise and fall of Uzziah in 2 **Chronicles 26** provides an excellent case study adapted from the John Maxwell Leadership Bible. Uzziah became king at the tender age of sixteen. He displayed robust, godly leadership and character in his formative years. He had the presence of mind to include among the people of influence a godly spiritual leader and mentor, Zachariah, who provided remarkable guidance and influence for the benefit of the young king. Uzziah pursued God, and the Lord prospered him. The Lord blessed him with military success and various other notable accomplishments. Here is the problem. As Uzziah's kingdom and wealth increased, so did his pride and arrogance, and he lost focus. His priorities shifted to personal success and fame rather than the things that delighted God's heart. His eyes drifted from God, and sin blinded his actions," and the rest is history.

Like many highly successful leaders today, Uzziah developed an attitude of superiority, and pride filled his heart. He assumed the priestly function by burning incense in the temple; a burning desire for power consumed his soul. The king stepped out of his God-ordained role to take on the priestly role. As a result, Uzziah left a legacy of disgrace. The Word of God says of him, "He dwelt in an isolated house because he was a leper; for he was cut off from the house of the Lord" (**2 Chronicles 26:21**), a sad ending to a promising start."

2.10 Fatigue and Discouragement

For the most part, a combination of fatigue and discouragement can become a silent and deadly cocktail of destruction and even death. The problem with fatigue and discouragement is that it is frequently hidden and is often the subconscious reason for inconsistent performance and obnoxious behavior. As a leader, you cannot afford to accommodate fatigue and discouragement. This is one of the primary reasons you cannot afford to ignore the promotion of others with whom to share responsibilities. This will help you sustain your physical, mental, and spiritual well-being and be of greater value to God and His kingdom in the long run.

This concept is greatly illustrated in the wise council given to Moses by his father-in-law.

> *"Moreover, you shall select from all the people able men, such as fear God, men of truth, hating covetousness; and place such over them to be rulers of thousands, rulers of hundreds, rulers of fifties, and rulers of tens. And let them judge the people at all times. Then it will be that every great matter they shall bring to you, but every small matter they shall judge. So it will be easier for you, for they will bear the burden with you. If you do this thing, and God so commands you, then you will be able to endure, and all these people will also go to their place in peace." So Moses heeded the voice of*

his father-in-law and did all that he had said. And Moses chose able men out of all Israel and made them heads over the people: rulers of thousands, rulers of hundreds, rulers of fifties, and rulers of tens. So they judged the people at all times; the hard cases they brought to Moses, but they judged every small case themselves." **Exodus 18:21-26**

Moses wisely sought counsel, and it's important that you do the same. Remember, sharing responsibilities with others can lighten your load and help prevent feelings of breakdown and isolation. You're not alone in this; reaching out can make a significant difference.

2.11 Addictions and Habits

I am well aware that this is somewhat debatable, especially if you are not well-informed, but the fact is, many spiritual leaders are hooked. Yes, I mean hooked on illegal substances such as alcohol and drugs. Others are hooked on gambling and sexual compulsions. This is to say there are specific psychological needs that have to be met. If, however, you will become a spiritually effective leader, these practices are unacceptable, and God has very little tolerance for such habits. It is no wonder now and again you hear of leaders being exposed. If you are addicted to any illegal substances or anything else for that matter—please be honest with yourself and seek help before it is too late. You should do everything you can to quit. This will allow the power of God to flow through you. It's essential to recognize that without a commitment to spiritual growth and repentance, you may feel distanced from your purpose or faith. Emphasizing a deep connection with God is crucial for personal development and fulfillment. Prioritizing this relationship can lead to positive changes and a renewed sense of direction.

2.8 Character Flaws

If you are going to increase your capacity to excel as a spiritually dynamic and effective leader, you must be of good character—no ifs, buts, or maybes. A.W. Tozer described the character as "the excellence of moral beings." As the excellence of gold is in its purity and the excellence of art is in its beauty, so is the excellence of man in his character once he is sold out to God. Persons of good character are noted for their honesty, ethics, and charity. Descriptions such as "man of principle" and "woman of integrity" assert character. A lack of character is a moral deficiency, and persons lacking character tend to behave dishonestly, unethically, and uncharitably." What, then, does the Bible say about Christian character? Character is defined as the strength of moral fiber. Internet Recommended Resource, "After You Believe, entitled, "Why Christian Character Matters" by N.T. Wright 2 explains.

> *A person's character is the sum of his or her disposition, thoughts, intentions, desires, and actions. It is good to remember that character is gauged by general tendencies, not on the basis of a few isolated actions. We must look at the whole life. For example, King David was a man of good character 1 Samuel 13:14 although he sinned on occasion 2 **Samuel 11**. And though King Ahab may have acted nobly once 1 Kings 22:35, he was still a man of overall bad character 1 Kings 16:33. Several people in the Bible are described as having noble character: Ruth (**Ruth 3:11**). Hanani and*

Hananiah Nehemiah 7:2, David Psalm 78:72, and Job 2:3. These individuals' lives were distinguished by consistent moral virtues. Your character is influenced and developed by your choices. Daniel "resolved not to defile himself" in Babylon (Daniel 1:8), and that godly choice was an important step in formulating an unassailable integrity in the young man's life. Character, in turn, influences our decisions. "The integrity of the upright guides them" (Proverbs 11:3a). Character will help us weather the storms of life and keep us from sin." (Read 9a). It is the Lord's purpose to develop character within us. "The crucible for silver and the furnace for gold, but the LORD test the heart" **Proverbs 17:3**. *Godly character is the result of the Holy Spirit's work of sanctification. Character in the believer is a consistent manifestation of Jesus in his life. It is the purity of heart that God gives, becoming purity in action. God sometimes uses trials to strengthen character: "We also rejoice in our sufferings, because we know that suffering produces perseverance; perseverance, character; and character, hope" Romans 5:3-4. The Lord is pleased when His children grow in character. "You test the heart and are pleased with integrity"* **1 Chronicles 29:17; Psalm 15:1-2**

We can develop character by controlling our thoughts Philippians 4:8, practicing Christian virtues 2 Peter 1:5-6, guarding our hearts Proverbs 4:23; Matthew 15:18-20, and keeping good company 1 Corinthians 15:33. Men and women of character will set a good example for others to follow, and their godly reputation will be evident to all. Titus 2:7-8.

Many established churches and successful private and public companies have been brought down to earth by capable leaders with questionable ethics. Recently, we've witnessed the public downfall of leaders from almost every area of society. One day, a leader can be a prominent, well-known, successful high flier; the next, he/she can fall into shame and disgrace. And while our outrage at disgraced leaders may be justified, we fail to realize how quickly the roles can be reversed, leaving us in their place.

The line between a successful leader and a disgraced failure is thinner than you can imagine. Fallen leaders never set out to sacrifice their integrity, abandon their ethical conduct, or exploit those they lead. But it happens! Their failure should serve as an example to us.

According to Mark Sanborn's "Why Leaders Fail," here are the following warning signs of leadership failure.

2.12 Losing Sight of What Is Important

Successful spiritual leaders are distinguished by their ability to aim high and to think outside the box. But often, as you lose sight of your goals, your aims and objectives become impaired. That will inevitably cause you to become side-tracked into:

- Trivial pursuits.

- Spending time with matters better left to others.

- Managing and controlling rather than "charting the course."

- Pursuit of selfish ambitions rather than that of the organization and the Kingdom of God.

- Becoming people pleasers rather than pleasing God.

- Preoccupied with the norm as opposed to innovation.

A leader's most significant influence stems from inner vision and integrity. Still, a leader can become fascinated with action and, in the process, lose touch with the all-important character development. I understand that juggling multiple tasks can feel overwhelming. However, higher levels of activity do not always translate into increased productivity. Take a moment to consider: what is your primary objective now? If you find it difficult to express this in a straightforward sentence, it may be a sign that your leadership could benefit from greater clarity. Remember, clarity can help you and your team stay focused and aligned.

There are several other reasons leaders fail, including the following;

2.13 Poor Communication

Losing sight of what is essential can disorient a leader and lead to poor communication. Followers can't possibly grasp a leader's intent when the leader isn't even sure what it is! Sometimes, leaders delude themselves into believing that committed followers can sense their goals and fulfill their wishes without being told. I may sometimes be guilty of this, because my preferred approach to leading people is to encourage them to take the initiative, but it doesn't always work that way; followers need to be told. When misunderstandings arise, leaders blame their people for lack of effort (or commitment) rather than recognizing their poor communication skills. "Say what you mean, and mean what you say" is timeless advice. Clarity of purpose is the starting point for all effective communication.

Please remember that when we talk about effective communication, we are not talking about the excellence of speech for those who do not possess that gift. We are discussing how to communicate your message clearly to avoid misunderstandings.

2.14 Fear of Failure

In most large organizations, leaders are pressured to be seen as successful by outperforming last year's success. In other words, past victories create pressure for leaders: "Will I be able to sustain outstanding performance?" The longer a leader is successful, the higher the perceived cost of failure. Leaders cannot take reasonable risks when driven by the fear of failure. They limit themselves to tried-and-proven methods. Attempts at innovation, the key to their initial success, diminish and eventually disappear. Whichever is more important to you: the journey or the destination? Are you still taking reasonable risks? Prudent leadership avoids reckless risk while refusing to be paralyzed by fear. A leader's credibility depends upon two qualities: what he or she does (competency) and who he or she is (character). Deficiencies in either area will result in an integrity problem. One of the highest principles of leadership is, therefore, integrity.

When a leader compromises on ethics, rationalizing it as necessary for the "greater good," he or she is on a slippery slope toward failure. All too often, leaders see their followers as merely a means to an end. They confuse manipulation with leadership. Such leaders rapidly lose the respect of followers. In an effort to maintain their image, they often transition from being insightful observers—"perceivers"—to passive admirers—"pleasers." They rely on their popularity to soothe the nagging guilt that arises from their compromised integrity. Reflect on this: are your beliefs aligned with your behavior, or are you compromising your values for acceptance?

2.15 Poor Self-Management

If a leader won't take care of himself, who else will? Nobody will notice signs of fatigue and stress unless he is blessed with unusually perceptive followers. Leaders are expected to perform and produce, but aren't superheroes with limitless energy. While leadership is stimulating, it is also exhausting. Like any other mortal, leaders are susceptible to feeling drained, depressed, and demotivated. Let me add here that those who neglect their physical, psychological, emotional, or spiritual needs are headed for disaster. Make time for refreshment and replenishment. Take care of yourself. Self-preservation isn't selfish; it's vital to the health and well-being of those you lead.

2.16 Loss of First Love

Leaders find themselves on the brink of crisis when they neglect their true passion for their role. The demanding nature of leadership, while often challenging, should ultimately bring a sense of fulfillment and joy. Embracing the journey should feel invigorating, allowing leaders to both inspire those around them and experience personal satisfaction in their efforts. In addition, leaders may also often experience frustration and a sense of futility when their responsibilities are disconnected from their dreams. To maintain motivation, it's essential for leaders to remain true to their passions and revisit the reasons that initially inspired them to embrace leadership. To ensure you stay aligned with your original inspiration, frequently ask yourself these three questions:

1. Why did I initially pursue leadership?

2. Have those reasons changed?

3. Do I still want to lead?

The various warning signs we encounter in life—ranging from vibrant stoplights directing traffic to carefully worded prescription labels—are designed with our well-being in mind. These signals serve as crucial safeguards, helping to shield us from potential disasters arising from negligence or misunderstanding. Disregarding these important clues would be nothing short of reckless. Therefore, it's essential to embark on a courageous self-examination, facing your truths without fear or hesitation.

Chapter Checklist

In Review

- There is no one alive who cannot increase their capacity to excel beyond the level of their thinking.

- Spiritual leaders are life transformers—they can excel as God-ordained.

- Your ability to solve problems equals success.

- If you will avoid failure, you must appreciate why leaders fail and develop strategies to deal with them. Here is a summary of the reasons.

  - Followers' expectations.

  - Selfishness and greed.

  - Failure to include others in the decision-making process.

  - Loneliness at the top.

  - Pride and arrogance.

  - Burnout and depression.

  - Addiction.

  - Character deficiencies.

  - Poor communication skills.

  - Fear of failure.

  - Poor self-management

  - Loss of first love/passion

Personal Notes

_____

_____

Chapter Three
SUCCESSFUL SPIRITUAL LEADERS ARE NOT SMARTER THAN YOU

Many individuals observe the impressive track records of successful leaders and conclude that these leaders possess some extraordinary qualities or skills that are absent in the average person. If this perspective aligns with your thoughts, I urge you to reconsider; your viewpoint may not be entirely accurate. The truth is, you also have the potential to reach remarkable heights of success.

> The pivotal distinction lies in recognizing that those who achieve their goals never leave it to luck or chance; instead, they devote significant time and effort to develop their skills, maintain a clear vision, and consistently pursue their ambitions with determination and purpose.

Believe it or not, you, too, have the potential to advance your leadership skills to the extent that you can leave a lasting mark among the greats of history. Pursuing this journey will demand your unwavering commitment, determination, and mastery of various essential disciplines. While these skills may seem challenging at first, they can be readily acquired with dedication and practice. Embrace the challenge, and you might find yourself standing alongside esteemed leaders who have changed the world.

Those who achieve their goals never leave it to luck or chance. They actively spent copious amounts of time advancing their skills...

Thomas Edison once said, "99% perspiration and 1% inspiration." It was encapsulated magnificently by Albert Einstein (the greatest modern-day physicist) when he was asked what the secret to his success was, particularly in quantum physics. His response was, "It's not that I am so smart; it's just that I stay with problems longer." The same is true of leadership. Successful spiritual leaders are not smarter than you in the sense that, as already indicated, they are not necessarily people with more significant academic advantage; neither are they people with more distinguished charismatic influence or superior oratorical skills. Although these are vital attributes, the critical difference is that these people are determined and committed to the cause. When unlocking your full leadership capabilities, you must release your treasure trove of heavenly wisdom to bring your life and ministry into God's plan for your destiny. In addition, you will also need to demonstrate a few basic but vitally essential policies, procedures, and principles that will enhance your ability to succeed.

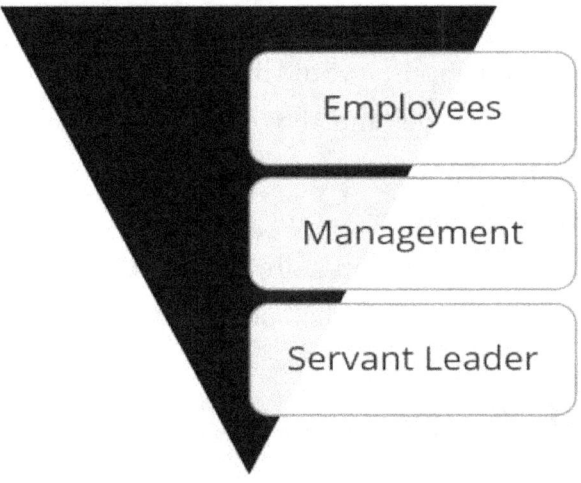

The bottom line is that human beings are always searching for ways to improve their skills and expand their mental capacity in every sector of life, and so should you. At this point, most of you may not have started on your leadership journey, or so you may think. As previously stated, anyone can be a leader, whether as a parent or an older sibling watching over younger siblings. Many individuals are starting their leadership journey for the first time and are excited about the opportunity for success. This is a great moment to explore strategies to enhance your skills and grow as a leader. Perhaps you are someone who has been around for a while and may have even received high awards for significant accomplishments. However, it's important to keep reaching for higher goals. Aim higher; your potential knows no bounds! In contrast, you may have been in your role for a long time without receiving any awards or recognition. To make matters worse, some of you might even believe that you do not deserve such honors. Whether you are a new leader, an experienced and successful professional, or someone who has been in the field without significant accomplishments, following the philosophical ideas in this book will captivate and revolutionize your leadership.

In the following paragraphs, I would like to discuss some vital character traits of a successful leader and show you how to achieve maximum effectiveness and position yourself for success by adopting these policies, procedures, and principles. I suggest you read through each point thoroughly, as it will help you fully understand and appreciate the principles taught in the rest of the book.

3.1 Successful Spiritual Leaders Are Servant Leaders

According to the scriptures, the primary reason for leadership success or failure is the difference between servant leadership and superstar leadership mentality. Superstar leaders are the type mentioned in the previous chapter, subsection one. They believe that a high position or a big title displays success and establishes their place in the kingdom. However, Jesus taught otherwise. **Matthew 20:20-28** explains;

Serving is Greatness

> *"Then the mother of Zebedee's sons came to Him with her sons, kneeling down and asking something from Him. And He said to her, "What do you wish?" She said to Him, "Grant that these two sons of mine may sit, one on Your right hand and the other on the left, in Your kingdom." But Jesus answered and said, "You do not know what you ask. Are you able to drink the cup that I am about to drink and be*

baptized with the baptism that I am baptized with?" They said to Him, "We are able." So He said to them, "You will indeed drink My cup, and be baptized with the baptism that I am baptized with; but to sit on My right hand and on My left is not Mine to give, but it is for those for whom it is prepared by My Father." And when the ten heard it, they were greatly displeased with the two brothers. But Jesus called them to Himself and said, "You know that the rulers of the Gentiles lord it over them, and those who are great exercise authority over them. Yet it shall not be so among you; but whoever desires to become great among you, let him be your servant. And whoever desires to be first among you, let him be your slave - just as the Son of Man did not come to be served, but to serve, and to give His life a ransom for many."

It is evidently clear that greatness does not come from having a fancy title or a high position. As Jesus taught, greatness comes through leaders who practice servanthood.

Servant Leadership

So what, then, is servant leadership? According to Wikipedia, "Servant leadership is a philosophy in which the leader's goal is to serve." This differs from traditional leadership, in which the leader's primary focus is the company's or organization's success. A Servant leader shares power and prioritizes the needs of those they serve, helping individuals grow and perform to their fullest potential. Instead of having people work to serve the leader, the leader exists to serve the people. According to its founder, Robert K. Greenleaf, a servant leader should focus on questions such as: "Do those being served grow as individuals? As they are served, do they become healthier, wiser, more autonomous, and more likely to become servants themselves?" When leaders embrace a servant leadership approach, they create a positive environment where both they and their followers can thrive. Those they lead experience personal growth, fostering greater commitment and engagement within the organization. As a result, the organization thrives. Since its introduction, several business organizations, including Starbucks and Marriott International, have embraced it as their primary leadership approach.

According to a 2002 study by Sen Sendjaya and James C. Sarros, servant leadership is practiced in some top-ranking companies. These companies excel largely due to their leadership style. Further research also confirms that servant leaders motivate their teams to go above and beyond the call of duty.

Servant leadership inspires followers and employees in the workplace to put forth their best effort to achieve the organization's goals, as they feel included and valued. It is clear that this leadership style has become increasingly popular since its introduction. Many organizations, drawn by its effectiveness and innovative approach, have since embraced this style as part of their management practices. It goes without saying that a spiritual leadership organization should be at the forefront, especially since this is a biblical principle. The key takeaway for you is to recognize the profound impact of servant leadership in creating a supportive and inclusive place of worship or work environment. By genuinely valuing and including followers and employees [in secular organizations], leaders can inspire them to give their best efforts toward achieving shared goals. Adopting the principles of servant leadership is a transformative approach that prioritizes the well-being and development of team members. It fosters a culture of empathy and support as leaders not only enhance employee engagement but also cultivate a strong sense of belonging and mutual respect within the organization. When team members feel genuinely acknowledged and valued for their contributions, they are more likely to flourish, leading to increased motivation and productivity. This positive dynamic ultimately enriches the entire organization, creating a thriving environment where everyone can succeed.

3.2 Understanding Servant Leadership

To fully grasp the concept of servant leadership, we can refer to the insights of Larry Spears, the Executive Director of the Robert K. Greenleaf Center for Servant-Leadership. In his description of servant leadership, he emphasizes four fundamental attributes.

1. Serving Others

Servant leadership is based on the core desire to serve others. Leaders prioritize the needs of the team and the organization over their own self-interest.

The philosophy is deeply rooted in fostering an environment where team members are inspired to reach their full potential. Servant leaders actively engage with their teams, adopting a nurturing approach that prioritizes their members' needs. By recognizing individual strengths and talents, these leaders cultivate a supportive atmosphere that encourages collaboration and empowers each team member to contribute meaningfully. This commitment to service ultimately paves the way for collective success as the team works harmoniously toward achieving the organization's goals.

2. Collaborative Work Ethic

An integrated work ethic genuinely embraces the relationships among individuals, organizations, and society, highlighting the profound importance of maintaining one's character and integrity in both personal and professional endeavors. Green-leaf's vision reflects a deep understanding that nurturing this approach not only enriches individual experiences but also contributes to the long-term success of organizations by enhancing performance. By fostering an environment where followers and employees feel free to express themselves, this ethic acknowledges and celebrates their unique traits and abilities, ultimately creating a more compassionate and cohesive environment.

3. Fostering a Sense of Community

Servant leadership focuses on fostering a sense of community among employees to achieve organizational goals. A community comprises individuals who share common social, economic, and political interests within a specific area or society.

Greenleaf emphasized that servant leaders play a crucial role in enhancing human well-being by nurturing a sense of community among their teams. He suggested that the actions and results of servant leaders are rooted in their commitment to creating a supportive and collaborative environment.

4. Shared Decision-Making Power

By sharing the decision-making power entrusted to them, servant leaders foster servant leadership in others. This theory suggests that the best way to achieve organizational success is to delegate power rather than hoard it. Power-sharing is achieved by developing employees' skills, promoting participation, and creating an empowering environment within the organization.

These actions foster a motivated workforce that is driven to achieve organizational objectives. Thus, the philosophy of servant leadership resembles an inverted pyramid, with servant leaders at the bottom and employees and other stakeholders at the top. This structure contrasts with the traditional hierarchical model of leadership.

3.2 Servant Leadership vs. Traditional Leadership

Servant leadership and traditional leadership are two contrasting philosophies, each with its own set of rules that yield different outcomes. Exploring these differences can provide valuable insights into how leadership styles reflect the core values that shape them. Servant leadership emphasizes the growth and well-being of individuals, prioritizing the needs of others above the leader's own interests. In contrast, traditional leadership focuses on hierarchical authority, where the leader's vision and directives drive the team or organization. Here are some key differences that might resonate with your own experiences and aspirations as a leader:

Servant Leadership	Traditional Leadership
Leaders focus on providing service to their team.	Leaders focus on improving productivity, business performance, and increasing market share.
Leaders encourage followers through personal growth opportunities, knowledge, and autonomy, without neglecting their development and well-being.	Leaders encourage employees to be productive through authority, guidance, and motivation.
Has more significant ethical implications for leadership.	It has fewer ethical implications for leadership.

Greenleaf also identified ten attributes of servant leadership, which are summarized below:

3.3 Attributes of Servant Leadership

1. Listening

Servant leaders excel at actively listening to the concerns that affect their followers, thereby improving communication and fostering deeper understanding. This commitment not only strengthens relationships but also empowers individuals to thrive collectively.

2. Empathy

A deeper understanding of team members enables servant-leaders to empathize with those they lead.

3. Healing

The healing attribute refers to the ability of servant leaders to create an environment that fosters a healthy organizational life balance, allowing followers or employees to heal from past undesirable personal and professional experiences. Healing provides wholeness to each team member.

4. Awareness

To enhance efficiency, servant leaders should actively recognize and reflect on their strengths and weaknesses. This self-awareness not only clarifies their role within the organization but also opens up valuable leadership opportunities. By embracing this understanding, they can promote a more effective and supportive environment for their team.

5. Persuasion

Servant leaders use influence and persistent persuasion techniques to achieve group consensus and drive team members toward organizational objectives. This contrasts with traditional leadership, which motivates team members through positive power and authority.

6. Conceptualization

Servant leaders possess a unique ability to anticipate challenges and develop innovative solutions for the issues that may arise within their teams, often before these problems are fully acknowledged.

Occupying a prominent position in the organizational hierarchy due to the authority bestowed upon them, they blend this power with a profound commitment to serving others. This dual role allows them to maintain a broader perspective, enabling them to clearly see the team's overall vision and dynamics. Their proactive approach not only encourages a supportive environment but also empowers team members, creating a space where collaboration and growth can thrive.

7. Foresight

To significantly enhance foresight, servant leaders and their team members should actively draw upon their rich reservoir of knowledge and experiences gained from past challenges. In addition, they should carefully analyze current trends and patterns to make informed, strategic decisions that anticipate and navigate the complexities of upcoming events.

8. Stewardship

The servant leaders' oversight extends from team members to the organization and to society at large. The stewardship attribute also entails servant leaders taking responsibility for team decisions and performances.

9. Commitment to the growth of people

Commitment is a fundamental aspect of servant leadership, where leaders demonstrate a sincere dedication to nurturing their team members' personal and professional development. This commitment is reflected in their willingness to invest time and resources in various initiatives aimed at growth. To effectively implement this vision, leaders often design and implement well-structured development programs alongside extensive organizational training sessions. These initiatives are designed to provide team members with valuable opportunities not only to refine their skills but also to broaden their knowledge. By fostering an environment of continuous learning and growth, these programs empower individuals to take meaningful steps forward in their roles, unlocking their full potential and paving the way for future advancement.

10. Building Community

Servant leaders emphasize the importance of nurturing strong, meaningful relationships among team members. By creating an environment of trust and open communication, they foster collaboration and enhance overall productivity. This approach not only elevates individual performance but also cultivates a lively and supportive community where, once again, everyone feels valued and engaged.

3 .4 Benefits of Servant Leadership

1. Stronger teams

Servant leaders cultivate a deep sense of respect and admiration by consistently supporting their team members. This dynamic enhances collaboration among teammates and encourages more productive behaviors. As a result, a harmonious team environment is created where individuals feel valued and connected. Ultimately, this approach strengthens the team, enabling it to achieve greater collective success.

2. Conducive working environment

Working alongside the leader in an organization fosters a positive work environment where interactions are more constructive and there is less competition to impress the leader through selfish political squabbles.

3. Alignment of personal and professional goals

A servant leader's support and encouragement for personal and professional development help team members align their objectives with the organization's goals. The alignment improves team members' engagement, commitment, and organizational loyalty, ultimately increasing growth and development.

4. Improved organizational agility

When leaders support their teams, those teams become more adaptable to change, fostering a truly agile organization.

Professional development supported by leaders augments team members' learning and development, strengthening strengths and addressing weaknesses.

5. Leadership training

Team members have the opportunity to grow and develop by working closely alongside their supportive servant leaders, who guide them every step of the way. This collaborative environment fosters a sense of responsibility and ownership, helping individuals to confidently enhance their leadership capabilities. Together, they create a nurturing space where everyone feels valued and empowered to reach their full potential.

6. Followers' motivation

Servant leadership has a remarkable capacity to elevate followers' motivation, igniting their courage to explore new ideas and unleash their creative potential. When leaders genuinely prioritize the personal and professional growth of their team members, they cultivate a dynamic and vibrant organizational culture. In this supportive environment, collaboration flourishes, diverse ideas are welcomed, and innovation thrives as team members feel empowered to take bold risks and share their unique perspectives.

7. People-oriented organizational culture

This philosophy nurtures a people-centered organizational culture that truly empowers and values each individual. We understand the importance of creating an environment where everyone feels respected and appreciated, enabling all team members to thrive and contribute their best.

8. Decreases Membership Turnover

When members and employees feel empowered, they are more likely to stay with the organization and actively contribute to its goals. This sense of empowerment creates a nurturing and supportive environment where individuals feel valued and appreciated. When people believe their contributions matter, they are motivated to collaborate, innovate, and strive for success. This heartfelt commitment ultimately helps the organization achieve its objectives. By fostering such a compassionate culture, the organization can build a dedicated, engaged, and deeply aligned team that feels connected to its mission and genuinely invested in each other's success.

Criticisms of Servant Leadership

Several critics, including Sendiaya and Sarros, have raised concerns regarding the origins of servant leadership theory. They contend that the true founder of this concept is Jesus Christ rather than Robert K. Greenleaf.

Their argument is underpinned by references to the Gospels authored by Matthew, Mark, Luke, and John in the Bible, illustrating the principles of servant leadership exemplified by Christ's teachings and actions. For those who know who Jesus is, this is sufficient for us. Even atheists recognize that the model of servant leadership, as taught by Christ, is the most effective form of leadership.

> This is sufficient for those who know who Jesus is. Even self-identified atheists agree that servant leadership, as taught by Christ, is the best form of   leadership.

3.5 Successful Leaders are Submissive to the Holy Spirit

Another critical factor in achieving success in spiritual leadership is the willingness to follow the guidance of the primary spiritual leader, the

"Holy Spirit." Embracing this leadership concept cultivates a deeper connection and ensures our actions align with a higher purpose. There's no doubt in my mind that if you are going to succeed in life (generally speaking), the principles of the kingdom must take precedence over everything else. This means total submission to the Holy Spirit. Summed up appropriately by Jesus Himself in (**Matthew 6.33**) "But seek first the kingdom of God and His righteousness, and all these things shall be added to you." John Maxwell refers to this as the "Motive Test." It would be best to do the right thing for the right reason. Leaders can easily get caught up in doing things for image's sake—after all, so many people are watching. Jesus warns us about facades and hypocrisy. This text is meant for everyone but has crucial implications for leaders. Jesus speaks about doing things to be seen by men rather than to please God (**Matthew 6:1).** He intends to produce God pleasers, not man pleasers. In other words, until you embrace the principles of the kingdom, you are wasting your time. If a spiritual leader is going to be effective, he must follow both the leadership and the directions of the Holy Spirit, even when it does not make sense. In **Genesis 12:1-4, God told Abraham to get out of his country, from his family and his father's house, to the** land that "I will show you. I will make you a great nation; I will bless you and make your name great, and you shall be a blessing. I will bless those who bless you and will curse the one who curses you, and in you, all the families of the earth shall be blessed."

Here is the point (verse 4), "So Abraham departed as the Lord had instructed him." Note that at this point, God did not tell Abraham where to go. God said, "Go, and I will show you." You see, my friends, sometimes it may not be clear which direction to take or what decision to make. However, every good leader should seek the Lord and submit to His leadership, ready to move at His instructions, even if that command seems bizarre. The Bible says this obedience was credited to Abraham's account as righteousness. And you know what the Bible says about righteousness? It exalts a nation. And if righteousness exalts a nation, how much more will it exalt you! Herein lies one of the primary reasons to seek the kingdom and its righteousness first.

A good leader exemplifies obedience to divine guidance and communicates with authority by saying, "thus says the Lord," as highlighted in **1 Kings 22:13-14**. This passage emphasizes the importance of aligning leadership actions and words with spiritual directives.

> *"The messenger that had gone to summon Micaiah said to him, 'Look, the word of the prophets with one accord is favorable to the kings; let your words be like one of them, and speak favorably.' But Micaiah said, 'As the Lord lives, whatever the Lord says to me, that I will speak.' When he had come to the king, the king said to him, 'Micaiah, shall we go to Ramoth-Gilead to battle, or shall we refrain?' He answered him, 'Go up and triumph; the Lord will give it into the hand of the king.'"*

As you can see, it is vital to ensure that you not only take hold of the kingdom in the first instance but also follow the Lord's instructions. Effective spiritual leadership demands submission to the Holy Spirit. "If you love me, keep My commandments" **John 14:15**. "If you keep My commandments, you will abide in My love, just as I have kept My Father's commandments and abide in His love" **John 15:10**. These scriptures make it abundantly clear that our obedience to His instructions demonstrates our love for God. Author Henry T. Blackaby, in his book ***"Experiencing God,"*** expertly stated,

> *"An obedience problem with God is a love problem with God. If we are to be Christ-led, we must be willing to obey regardless of the cost. Obedience consists of three components: (1) Timeliness (act or speak when the Lord indicates, not before and not after), (2) Fullness (partial obedience is disobedience), and (3) Joyfulness (not grumbling, complaining, whining, etc.). Without these essential ingredients, success will be difficult to achieve."*

3.6 Successful Leaders are Visionaries

In the previous paragraphs, I mentioned servanthood and submission to the Holy Spirit as two of the most significant qualities of effective leadership. However, I must emphasize that successful leaders are distinguished by their ability to envision a compelling future and inspire others to work towards it. Visionary leadership involves:

1. **Clear Vision**: They articulate a clear and inspiring vision that serves as a roadmap for the future.

2. **Inspiration**: They motivate and energize their team, fostering a sense of purpose and shared goals.

3. **Innovation**: Visionary leaders embrace innovation, encouraging creativity and new ideas to drive progress.

4. **Strategic Thinking**: They think strategically, anticipating challenges and opportunities and adapting their plans accordingly.

5. **Long-term Focus**: They maintain a long-term perspective, ensuring that current actions align with future objectives.

By embodying these qualities, visionary leaders guide their organizations toward sustainable success and growth. The vision to which I am alluding can only be acquired by fully embracing the will, purpose, and guidance of the Holy Spirit. The foundation of effective leadership lies in developing a well-defined plan. This plan should be rooted in a compelling vision that inspires and motivates others, and in a strategic approach that outlines the specific steps needed to achieve our goals. Combining these elements is not just important; it is vital for navigating the complexities of leadership and ensuring meaningful success.

Leadership is fundamentally about guiding people. For instance, as a parent, your role is to lead your children. If you are a manager, your responsibility is to lead your employees, although there is a significant difference between being a manager and a leader, which I will discuss in more detail in a later chapter. Similarly, if you are a church leader, your role is to guide your congregation. Since effective leadership involves supervising people, it is essential to have a clear plan to lead them successfully. Whether your goal is to provide your child with the best education or to explore what life is like in Antarctica during the winter, you will need a well-thought-out plan of action to achieve your objectives.

To embellish this point, in the case of spiritual leadership, not only do you need to have a plan, but as stated, you must also have a vision. From a Scriptural perspective, every great leader begins his journey with a vision. Your vision motivates you; what drives you to persevere when the going gets tough? Your vision is the goal you so desperately need to accomplish. It is a picture of what things will be like in the future. A successful leader cannot live out the vision he doesn't have. And his organization can go no further than the vision set before them. That's why Scripture tells us to: "Write the vision and make it plain on tablets." **(Habakkuk 2:2)**. The vision must be written down in black and white as a constant reminder so everyone is on the same page. In other words, the vision is "the blueprint for building a bridge to the future" for an appointed time. **Habakkuk 2:3** explains, "For the vision is yet for an appointed time, but in the end, it will speak, and it will not lie. Though it tarries, wait for it because it will surely come; it will not tarry."

The point is that leaders with no vision cannot be considered leaders at all. Leaders who are satisfied with the status quo or are more concerned with survival than growth will fail to make an impact. The most effective leaders are unconventional, inspired, focused, and resourceful. In another way, they have the skill and imagination to create change and invent new things. The alternative is to build unresponsive organizations, which only sets you up for failure. You must focus on your followers' satisfaction and loyalty as part of your vision. You must find ways to engage and incorporate them into your innovation and planning initiatives. Your leadership days are numbered if you ignore, mistreat, or fail to value your followers.

3.7 Successful Leaders Understand Their Mission

A successful leader must not only have a vision but must possess a clearly defined mission. A leader who does not spell out his mission will lead aimlessly and without direction. "A leader's mission can be communicated unofficially or officially. Unofficial communications in this regard are those in which leaders explain verbally to their followers what their organization does, why it does it, and how it does it." An official manifestation is written on paper, usually as a mission statement, and serves as a physical reference point for all to see.

According to Author Don Miller, a great mission statement should identify three things:

1. Your skills/abilities

2. Your traits, and

3. Your values, dreams, and passions.

These three things identify what is essential, so you can focus on those things.

Miller suggests considering the following when putting your statement together.

- What is your plan?

- What's essential, and why are you here?

- Must have the courage to live a life true to you and not for someone else!

- It should tell you what you are not.

- Your core values need to be reflected in the statement.

- It should be practical for today and lead to the future.

- It should act like a filter for you, guiding your decisions.

- Make it visible and leave room for subtle adjustments.

- It will keep you from doing things that are not important or ineffective.

Take the next few days to craft a thoughtful personal mission statement. This may require some time and introspection, but the insights you gain will profoundly shape your approach to leadership. Please take this opportunity to reflect on your values, aspirations, and the legacy you wish to create, as it can inspire those around you!

3.5 Successful Leaders Set Goals

Setting goals tells you what you want and how you will achieve it. If you do not have an aim, you could end up anywhere. More importantly, you have the power to set your goals wherever you want, and with that, you can aim high. You can aim for the stars! Don't settle for second best. With God's help, the sky is the limit to what you can achieve. As the scripture says, "If you can believe, all things are possible to them that believe" **Mark 9:23**.

One word of caution: please do not set unreachable goals or goals that are too easy to achieve. Your goal should be set at a level that provides a challenge but is attainable with some effort. Once again, you can achieve anything you want; all you need to know is how. And as a servant leader, your success is determined by how much you are connected to and devoted to Christ. In other words, the more you understand who you are in Him, the greater your chances of success. "The degree to which you abide in Him depends upon the depth of your understanding of His love, power, grace, faithfulness, mercy, compassion, patience, peace, and joy. As His child, friend, brother, bride, beloved, you and I are in Christ, and He is in us." According to **Ephesians 1:3,** He has bestowed upon us every spiritual blessing in heavenly places in Christ. The deeper our understanding of these concepts, the more significant our achievements will be, ultimately increasing our likelihood of reaching our goals. Deepening our understanding equips us to navigate challenges and seize opportunities.

3.6 Successful Leaders are Masters of the Art of Influence

To be an effective leader, you must be able to influence others to support and implement decisions that you, together with your followers, perceive as necessary. With influence, leadership is effective. In other words, one of the primary purposes of leadership is to influence outcomes. Therefore, if you have no impact on the result of a given undertaking, you are wasting your time.

Influence involves people as well as things or events. Its strength and effectiveness can also vary. The process the leader uses to influence someone or something can take various forms.

Webster's dictionary describes influence as "the power to change or affect someone or something: the power to cause changes without directly forcing them to happen: A person or thing that affects someone or something in an important way."

Influence is, therefore, "a force one person (the agent) exerts on someone else (the target) to induce a change in the target, including changes in behaviors, opinions, attitudes, goals, needs, and values," and "the ability to affect the behavior of others in a particular direction."

3.6.1 How a Leader Exerts Influence

To exert influence, a leader uses strategies, techniques, or actual behaviors designed to change another person's attitudes, beliefs, values, or actions. Leaders tend to use different approaches and have somewhat different objectives depending on the desired outcome of the influence. For instance, this is often seen when a leader attempts to influence someone above or below them.

An indispensable reason for choosing a specific influence technique may be the leader's preferences. For example, a church leader may want to influence followers to:

- Gain support for a specific project.

- Make adjustments to their plans and schedules.

- Approve and support the leader's plans and proposals.

- Accept and carry out new assignments.

- Provide relevant and on-time information.

- Discontinue inappropriate behavior.

- Increase their commitment toward a goal.

- Influence the outcome of a decision.

- Increase awareness to get something done.

Types of Influence Techniques

3.6.2 The Power Use Model

According to Anita Hall, Extension Educator, and Laverne Barrett, Extension Leadership Specialist, University of Nebraska–Lincoln Extension Publications Index: Communities and Leadership development Issued March 2007, the Power Use Model predicts someone's choice of influence techniques in terms of their;

1. Softness, versus

2. Hardness.

This dimension is defined by how much freedom a technique gives individuals to decide whether to yield or resist an influence attempt: Hard tactics leave individuals with less freedom than soft tactics. Hard tactics include pressure, assertiveness, upward appeal, and title designation. These behaviors are perceived as more forceful and push the person to comply. From a leadership perspective, I do not approve of hard tactics. Soft tactics, on the other hand, influence behaviors that are considered thoughtful and constructive. Soft tactics include "personal appeal," "consultation," "inspirational appeal," and "rational persuasion."

Soft tactics allow the person to be influenced with greater flexibility in deciding whether to accept the influence than hard tactics do. Hard influence tactics can strain the relationship between the leader and the follower, especially when the action is unnecessary.

Influence techniques can also be divided into "push" and "pull" tactics. Both categories can get results. Push tactics get short-term results, while pull tactics gather support rather than compliance.

Mastering the art of influence is a crucial component of leadership. A successful leader will understand which influence technique works best for the situation and the person or group. Therefore, you must ensure the correct method is used; otherwise, the desired results may not be achieved. Effective leadership and influence require a wide array of techniques. Too often, potential leaders use the same technique repeatedly, getting little results because they apply it inappropriately. Leaders must learn the art of influence if their ideas are to be accepted in support of a given change.

3.7 Successful Leaders are Effective Team Builders

To influence team members effectively, leaders must create a positive climate where followers feel genuinely motivated to contribute and support the leader. It's essential that team members feel heard, appreciated, and truly part of a cohesive unit. This sense of belonging and recognition fosters a deeper connection among the team. Creating this positive climate requires critical skills that help leaders earn their followers' respect and trust. By showing empathy and understanding, leaders can recognize individual contributions and challenges, making team members feel valued in their unique roles. This approach not only enhances motivation but also strengthens the overall team dynamic, allowing everyone to thrive together.

Kay H. Roman of collegiateproject.com stated that five critical team leadership skills will help leaders effectively influence and demonstrate respect for their team members.

1. Understanding behavioral styles

2. Listening and effectively communicating

3. Giving praise

4. Handling disputes with care

5. Use problem-solving and persuasion instead of criticism.

A leader must spend valuable time on team building because no man is an island. Success cannot be achieved without the combined effort of individuals working together. More importantly, by creating teams, you should leverage the diversity of talents within your organization.

The importance of a sturdy foundation cannot be overstated when constructing a house, be it a towering skyscraper that pierces the skyline or a quaint cottage nestled among the trees. Just as every building requires a solid foundation to ensure stability and longevity, effective leadership is built on essential principles that underpin a successful structure. The seven core principles discussed earlier provide the necessary support, creating a reliable framework for exemplary leadership to flourish.

3.8 Successful Leaders Invest in Those They Lead

According to Mike Myatt, Chief Strategy Officer and N2growth of "Share and Enjoy": Effective spiritual leaders are fully committed to investing in those they lead. They support their team, build into it, mentor and coach it, and truly care for it. Leaders who have not fully invested in their teams won't have a team – at least not an effective one. One thing, though, is that leaders can invest only in followers who are committed and submissive, in the sense that they allow their leader to lead them, not in those who think they should lead their leaders or resist authority.

Influential leaders are accountable. They do not blame others or claim credit for their team's success but always accept responsibility for failures on their watch. Most of all, good leaders are responsible for their team. It is said, "Leaders not accountable *to* their people will eventually be held accountable *by* their people."

Leaders who are not intentional and focused will fail themselves and their team. Leaders who lack discipline will model the wrong behaviors and inevitably spread themselves too thin. Organizations are at greatest risk when leaders lose focus.

Each of these critical team leadership skills builds upon the other. Recognizing behavior helps team leaders more effectively listen to and respond to team members. Giving praise and accepting criticism effectively helps team leaders earn respect. Involving people using a problem-solving style helps engage them and demonstrates respect for their knowledge and experience. Finally, using problem-solving and persuasion instead of criticism helps team leaders positively influence behavior.

Fostering a positive team climate is crucial for establishing and nurturing trust among team members. When individuals feel supported and valued in a collaborative environment, they are more likely to trust one another and their leader. This trust is essential for enhancing communication, encouraging creativity, and promoting a sense of belonging. As a result, teams that operate with a strong foundation of trust are more effective in achieving their goals and navigating challenges together.

3.9 A Successful Spiritual Leader is a Strategist

According to Sheri Cyprus of the Strategic Leadership Institute, based at P.O. Box 14137, Sino Ville, Pretoria 0129, strategic leadership is the art of applying strategic thinking to personnel management. This approach emphasizes the essential role of motivating team members, encouraging them to take the initiative and actively contribute to the organization's success. In this leadership style, the leader's primary strategy is to inspire followers to contribute more to the organization, fostering an environment where creativity and proactivity thrive. The process involves deep reflection and careful planning, where thoughtful strategies are developed to address future challenges. A successful leader not only directs but also empowers others to recognize their potential and take meaningful actions to equip and uplift followers.

3.9.1 Implementation of Strategy

Strategic leaders always look ahead and analyze the present to prepare for what may be ahead for their ministries. Awareness is arguably a key part of a strategic leadership style, but it must be followed by well-thought-out action. Strategic leaders are adaptable and growth-oriented. They take responsibility for getting things done by training followers to think and act more effectively, achieving the best possible results for the organization.

One of the main goals of strategic leadership is a positive outcome. Yet it's not merely about increasing time spent, but about its strategic efficiency and working harder for the organization's best interests. Although the strategic leadership style always keeps the organization's best interests in mind, it also appreciates the followers' unique talents, gifts, and efforts.

As with soft tactics, strategic leaders use leadership techniques that empower and motivate rather than dictate to followers. Another goal of strategic leadership is to create an environment in which followers anticipate the organization's needs regarding their roles. Followers in a ministry led by a strategic leader are encouraged to take the initiative. Strategic leaders reward servanthood and commitment by promoting them and offering incentives to support the ministry's success.

Strategic leaders are always very flexible in their approach. For instance, if it doesn't make sense to appoint someone to a leadership position or to initiate other changes, a strategic leader will reconsider the situation rather than proceed. Careful planning before taking action is crucial for the strategic style of leadership. The philosophy behind this practice is to strategize in every aspect of decision-making. This is because a more thoughtful leadership approach can lead to tremendous success in any ministry. It's essential to recognize that a commanding approach, where orders are shouted at followers, is far from practical in leadership. Instead, adopting a coaching style is much more beneficial. This method emphasizes guidance and support, allowing leaders to foster an environment where collaboration thrives. Moreover, strategic leadership -- the intrinsic potential of followers, valuing their input and encouraging them to play an active role in decision-making processes. By considering team members' perspectives and ideas, leaders not only empower their followers but also foster a more inclusive and dynamic environment for growth and innovation.

3.10 Successful Leaders Operate in a Spirit of Humility.

I cannot emphasize this point too strongly. To become a successful leader, humility is one of the most important qualities you need. And as pointed out before, the spirit of humility must be accompanied by a willingness to serve others. Humility will cause people to follow you because they want to, not because they must. Remember: "Rules without relationship cause rebellion," while genuine humility and spiritual leadership attract others like nothing else. People want to follow those who willingly serve alongside them and set an example. At the age of seventeen, I experienced my first personal example of this. I was appointed chairperson for the local community council in our local district in Westmoreland, Jamaica, where I grew up. Back then, in December, the local government would assign paid community work to residents. As the chairperson of the community council, I was automatically given the job of supervising the project. I instinctively joined the workers and performed the assigned duties as though I were one of them. Not that I understood the principle of servant leadership at the time, but I noticed how deeply appreciative the workers were.

Consequently, they gave their best to please me—the outcome was astounding. Fellow workers will always respond positively to a servant's attitude.

One of the main reasons humility is so vital is that "God opposes the proud but gives grace to the humble **(James 4:6; 1 Peter 5:5)**. What, then, is pride in the context of spiritual leadership? Pride is simply the belief that "I (we) can build the church without the involvement of the Holy Spirit. On the other hand, humility is the belief that "apart from Him, I (we) can do nothing" **(John 15:5)**. In essence, it is the heartfelt belief that it is impossible for us to lead effectively and in a way that reflects His love and brings Him glory, without allowing Him to take control.

In addition, humility is a spirit that tells you others are more important than you are. It was said of Moses, the leader of over 2.5 million people, "Now Moses was a very humble man, more humble than anyone else on the face of the earth" **(Numbers 12:3)**. Thinking too highly of yourself prevents you from genuinely caring for others. Humility enables you to serve wholeheartedly and sets an example of love that influences others to follow.

3.11 Successful Leaders are People of Integrity

Finally, a spiritual leader is a person of integrity. People do not want to follow someone they do not respect. Speaking to servants, **Ephesians 6:6-8** tells us: "Obey them not only to win their favor, when their eyes are on you, but like slaves of Christ doing the will of God from your heart. Serve wholeheartedly, as if you were serving the Lord, not men, because you know that the Lord will reward everyone for whatever good he does, whether slave or free."

Moreover, effective spiritual leadership inherently relies on honesty. When individuals sense a lack of trustworthiness, they are likely to turn away from both the leader and their message. This principle is poignantly illustrated in Proverbs 16:13, which states, "Kings take pleasure in honest lips; they value a man who speaks the truth." This scripture underscores the profound importance of integrity in leadership, highlighting that sincerity not only fosters trust but also enhances a leader's influence and ability to connect with others.

Chapter Checklist

In Review

- Successful spiritual leaders never leave it to chance.

- Success is 99% perspiration and 1% inspiration.

- Successful spiritual leaders are not necessarily more intelligent than you because they are not necessarily people with more outstanding academic advantages/qualifications.

- Successful spiritual leaders are submissive to the Holy Spirit.

- Successful spiritual leaders move as God commands and speak what the Lord says.

- Successful spiritual leaders have a plan, a vision, and a strategy to accomplish that plan.

- Effective spiritual leaders focus on followers' satisfaction and loyalty.

- Effective spiritual leaders understand their mission.
- Effective spiritual leaders are goal-oriented (setters).
- Effective spiritual leaders are masters of the art of influence.
- Effective spiritual leaders are effective team builders
- Effective spiritual leaders invest in those they lead.
- Effective spiritual leaders are strategists.
- Effective spiritual leaders are servant leaders.
- Effective spiritual leaders lead with a spirit of humility.
- Successful spiritual leaders lead with integrity.

Personal Notes

Chapter Four
THE MATURITY PROCESS

Maturity plays a crucial role in shaping effective leaders as they pursue leadership success. It is not just an option; it is a vital component that distinguishes great leaders from good ones. Embracing the maturity process allows leaders to draw upon the wisdom gained from their experiences, cultivate patience through challenges, and develop humility by recognizing and accepting their limitations. In essence, maturity significantly enhances a leader's effectiveness and inspires those around them to strive for greater advancement.

As leaders, the journey to maturity is like refining precious metals—challenging and uncomfortable but incredibly rewarding. It demands a profound internalization of values, a strong commitment to personal growth, and an unwavering dedication to the well-being of those you lead. Embracing this path empowers you to become more effective and impactful as a leader.

This chapter will examine the hypothesis supporting the maturity process, emphasizing how and why leaders should embrace the challenges with grace and resilience. This concept underscores the significance of self-awareness, emotional intelligence, and the enduring pursuit of wisdom. By understanding and committing to this process, leaders can inspire trust, promote meaningful relationships, and create lasting impact.

Welcome to "The Maturity Process," where we unravel the mystery of the essential journey every leader must undertake to truly thrive and lead with purpose.

1.0 Sacrifice

Successful spiritual leadership calls for great sacrifices, and all great leaders willingly sacrifice all for their people. Nelson Mandela, one of the greatest icons of the Twentieth Century, once said, 'Real leaders must be ready to sacrifice all for the freedom of their people.' Dedicating his life to the struggle for freedom and equality, Mandela believed that being free was "not merely to be free from incarceration (imprisonment), but to live in a way that respects and enhances the freedom of others."

As someone who spent a significant part of his life in prison, Mr. Mandela managed to preserve his faith despite the cruelty of human nature. He had a heart that could overcome any circumstances a leader faced. He firmly believed that life is full of challenges and that "after climbing a great hill, one only finds that there are many more hills to climb." Mandela went on to say, ''There is nothing like returning to a place that remains unchanged to find how you have altered."

Despite his numerous life challenges, the late South African Leader considered himself an optimist. As a leader, you, too, are to be positive in the face of opposition and trials. "Part of being optimistic is keeping one's head pointed toward the sun, one's feet moving forward. There were many dark moments when my faith in humanity was sorely tested, but I would not and could not give myself up to despair. That way lies defeat and death." (**Nelson Mandela**)

As one of the most prominent philosophers of the 20th century, Mandela believed that true leaders are to be modest shepherds of their people. The man, who sacrificed his whole life in fighting apartheid, racism, and inequality, also said, "No matter what challenges and downfalls one faces on life's journey, the only way forward is to stand up, overcome your fear, and be ready for the next trial."

To become a successful spiritual leader, you must make significant sacrifices and embrace a rigorous journey that demands great endurance, much like Nelson Mandela's disposition during and after his trials.

In his book, *The 21 Irrefutable Laws of Leadership,* John Maxwell stated, "*We must give up, to go up,*" and that our call to lead "is no cakewalk" but calls for responsibility and sacrifice. John Maxwell added that when leadership becomes more difficult and requires increasing sacrifice, it gives leaders a chance to evaluate their motives. We can observe this principle throughout the length and breadth of the Bible. For example, Jeremiah was called to be the minister of opposition. He was probably one of the most unpopular prophets. His message was not what the people wanted to hear, and, as a result, they responded by subjecting him to beatings and punishment. He was treated worse than most criminals, imprisoned in a dungeon, and nearly suffocated in a dry well for preaching the gospel. In addition, as part of his calling, he was not permitted to marry.

You, too, may have to endure some hardships, but it may be what God requires to get you to the place He wants. Let me assure you that no matter how difficult the journey may become, you can take comfort in the knowledge that God has called you to fulfill His purpose. With unwavering faith in your mission, you can be confident that, in due time, you will reap the fruits of your hard work and dedication, leading you to undeniable success.

The list of problems facing us in the 21st century is daunting. From climate change to waste management, social inequality, public health issues, extreme poverty, pedophilia on the increase, media corruption, war in the Middle East and other places around the world, and international threats, including disease epidemics such as Ebola. Then you have disintegrations and disruptions caused by globalization, and the list continues. "Humanity's survival will depend on leadership that can "chart a course" through an uncertain and turbulent sea of constant change." We can no longer afford to sit back and wait for a great leader to emerge to take the helm. As believers, we must take responsibility for effective spiritual leadership in our own little corners of the world.

The aggregate effect of these small, effective facets of transformational leadership can mobilize the Body of Christ to become champions of the cause of Christ. The good news is that with a little effort, we can all become influential leaders. Remember, the kingdom of God here on earth is built by reaching one person at a time, Jesus being the Chief Master Builder. By applying effective leadership techniques, we can create a strong, enduring, and magnificent edifice [spiritually speaking]. If this is to be accomplished, the following rules apply:

- **Put people first**. People are the most valuable asset of any organization. The U.S. military's motto is "Mission first, People always." This is an explicit recognition that nothing can be accomplished without people.

- **Emphasize honesty and integrity.** The most technically competent leaders who lack honesty and integrity are nothing more than impostors. If a church group is to thrive and endure, it must cultivate trust, beginning with its leaders. However, the organization's integrity ultimately depends on the combined honesty and integrity of every member.

- **Encourage leaps of faith and innovation.** Organizations that stick to tradition are bound to stagnate and ultimately fail. Progress comes only through moving into unexplored territories and trying out new things. Therefore, it would be necessary to identify and reward faith-takers and innovators in your organization.

- **Embrace change.** Change is a constant in life—in fact, it is the only constant. To be an effective leader, you should not only embrace change but also promote it.

- **Foster a learning environment.** Science and technology have been increasing rapidly in each new decade, which means that learning needs to be a life-long pursuit. In addition to continually upgrading yourself, as a leader, you should encourage your followers to upgrade their skills and knowledge regularly.

- **Establish open communication.** Information is the key to power and success. As a leader, you must have access to the knowledge of those around you. An atmosphere of open, unbiased communication provides the knowledge to make effective decisions.

As a leader, it's important to remember that your current position is not your final destination. We all have the potential to achieve greater things, and it's okay to reach for the stars, knowing that higher heights and deeper depths are out there waiting for you to discover. The journey can be challenging, but the idea of "deep calling to deep" reminds us to dig deeper—not just in our commitment but also in our understanding of the word of God.

You must also understand the importance of keeping your vision fresh and relevant. By ensuring your team is consistently informed and updated, you help create a sense of unity and purpose that moves everyone forward together. It's about fostering an environment where everyone feels involved and motivated to contribute to the common goal. Remember, you're not alone on this journey; your team is with you every step of the way.

4.1 The Processing

Spiritual leadership success is synonymous with those who have endured a challenging processing period. You are not expected to gain true success until you have gone through a progression of hardening operations. Whether you like it or not, this is part of the journey and is not expected to be a great expedition. But despite the challenges, it's a journey worth cherishing in that it carries excellent rewards for success. For instance, it is designed to make you stronger, test your endurance, re-shape your character, increase your value, reinforce your sense of purpose, establish yourself, and give you perspective. In other words, it is intended to develop who and what you are becoming. This will help you gain a deeper understanding of your mission, core values, and inherent strengths, and identify areas that may need further development. Additionally, it offers clarity on the changes that are necessary for your growth and empowers you to engage in the experience and practice of new skills, fostering personal and professional transformation.

This idea is further amplified by John Maxwell, who said that leadership is an ongoing process on the inside and the outside. Leadership development is not a one-time venture; it should be a lifelong process of continuous growth.

The external aspect of leadership development includes the physical and mental skills and capabilities needed to lead your followers in a particular circumstance. The more competent leaders are, the more respect they will get from their followers.

The internal aspect of leadership development is about transformation through the development of character qualities. For example, the more you follow through to do what you say you will do, the more trust you will gain from followers. While particular skill development may vary by function and situation, the character-building aspect of leadership is a principle. Therefore, no matter the skills needed to lead a team, the foundation of any leadership program is building character qualities. Here are four cornerstone qualities for trans-formational leadership development.

1. Spiritual Discernment

2. Responsibility

3. Integrity, and

4. Trustworthiness

Influential spiritual leaders should strive to develop their ideal selves. Successful leaders recognize their own limitations and actively seek to address them. They prioritize the continuous enhancement of both their personal and social competencies, as well as their technical skills. This ongoing development not only helps them grow as individuals but also enables them to inspire and guide their teams more effectively. By embracing a lifelong learning mindset, they ensure they are well-equipped to navigate challenges and foster a collaborative environment.

4.2 Spiritual Discernment

Every spiritual leader must embrace the practice of spiritual discernment and develop a profound awareness of their inner selves. This is essential for guiding others on their spiritual journeys effectively. The more spiritually discerning you are, the better you will understand others. And, the better you know people, the better you can lead them. In addition, it will help you use wisdom when delivering feedback or gauging someone's understanding or emotional response to a conversation. Those with very little spiritual discernment tend to deny, avoid difficult conversations, justify their abrasive behavior in external circumstances, and resort to manipulation instead of honesty.

In fact, you can only be as honest as your self-awareness. To paraphrase author Gary Zukav of <u>Seat of the Soul</u>, "If you are not aware of your intention before an interaction, you will become aware of your intention afterward." The more aware you become of your thoughts and emotions, the greater your ability to respond thoughtfully rather than simply reacting in the moment.

This mindful approach paves the way for developing the next important character quality. Keep in mind that experiencing spontaneous reactions is a perfectly normal part of being human. These instinctive responses can arise unexpectedly in various situations. However, with dedicated practice and thoughtful self-reflection, you can develop a greater awareness of your emotions and behaviors. This enhanced understanding will not only enrich your relationship with yourself but will also lead to more meaningful and authentic interactions with those around you.

4.3 Responsibility

Understanding the importance of responding rather than reacting is crucial for effective leadership and healthy relationships in any organization. Responsibility is about self-management and owning up to problems. In other words, as a leader, you are responsible and have your followers' backs. Here are several compelling reasons why leaders should care about this concept:

1. **Enhanced Communication**: By fostering a culture of response over reaction, communication improves significantly among team members. For example, when a leader takes time to respond thoughtfully to feedback or criticism rather than reacting defensively, it en-

courages open dialogue. This, in turn, creates an environment where team members feel valued and heard, leading to stronger collaboration.

2. **Decreased Drama and Conflict**: As highlighted in Marlene Chism's insights, focusing on responsibility helps reduce unnecessary drama in the workplace [or among followers]. Imagine a team facing a setback; a leader who blames others can create a tense atmosphere. In contrast, a leader who takes ownership and explores solutions fosters a more resilient team that learns from mistakes, ultimately enhancing morale and fruitfulness.

3. **Personal and Professional Growth**: Embracing the idea of response over reaction encourages personal development. Leaders who practice self-management and recognize their triggers can set a positive example for their followers. This transformative approach not only benefits the leader but also inspires team members to develop similar skills, leading to a more empowered team.

4. **Building Trust and Loyalty**: When leaders demonstrate responsibility, they nurture trust within their teams. For instance, a leader who admits their mistakes and actively seeks input for improvement creates an atmosphere of loyalty and respect. Team members are more likely to commit to a leader who is transparent and accountable, enhancing overall team cohesion.

5. **Effective Problem-Solving**: A leader who takes ownership of challenges is better positioned to devise successful strategies. Consider a project that falls behind schedule; a reactive leader may focus on assigning blame, while a responsive leader would analyze the situation, gather input, and collaborate with the team to find solutions. This proactive approach not only addresses immediate concerns but also strengthens

the team's problem-solving capacity for the future.

6. **Long-Term Cultural Shift**: When leaders prioritize responsible responses, they can drive a cultural shift within their organization that emphasizes growth, learning, and accountability. Over time, this fosters a sustainable environment where team members feel motivated to contribute positively, ultimately benefiting the organization as a whole. By acknowledging and actively addressing the tendency to overreact, individuals and leaders can create an environment that promotes well-being and productivity. This approach encourages open communication, reduces misunderstandings, and cultivates stronger relationships among team members. As a result, members feel more valued and engaged, which significantly contributes to the organization's overall success and performance. By prioritizing this practice, team members can become thriving communities where every individual has the chance to excel.

4.4 Integrity

It has been said that "Integrity is the alignment of your thoughts, words, and actions." You can tell you aren't acting from a place of integrity when what you say you are committed to doing does not align with your actions. As a leader, you must know your hidden intentions and competing agendas. For example, you may say you are committed to team building, but you have one follower who needs some straight talk. So, as a leader, you know the possible outcome is likely to cause an upset; however, you certainly don't want to rattle the follower, who happens to be one of your most committed followers. This is referred to as "two competing agendas." On the one hand, you want the team to work together, but that requires a serious conversation. Would you rather ignore the situation to keep that follower happy? This is known as the "integrity gap." Your people know when you are off course, but it is up to you to have the courage to maintain your integrity in each situation.

4.5 Reliability

Many leaders lack reliability, and one major telltale sign is inconsistency. As previously mentioned, this means you do not always do what you say you will do. But if you are going to lead effectively, you must do as you say. This means you are predictable. "Predictability makes followers feel safe as the brain craves a certain amount of certainty."

Another quality that can make people feel safe is the ability to speak to you without making you feel flustered or acting unreasonably. It means you must also learn to master your energy, especially your emotions.

You can develop leadership skills tailored to your needs, but the principles must be thoroughly understood. If they are not appreciated, they may also not be willing to adapt. In other words, you will experience difficulty due to a lack of support. Followers may not be seen to be taking responsibility or showing integrity and reliability because they lack understanding.

Questions for Reflection

- What might other people know about me that I don't know about myself?

- Am I demonstrating patterns of complaining, shifting blame, or making excuses in any part of my life?

- Is there any place in my leadership role where I have a hidden agenda or conflicting priorities?

- Do people feel safe around me?

Not everyone is willing to go through the process—it is a crucial time, as it requires a great deal of patience and is the part most leaders despise. Everyone is in a rush to reach the goal, but the process is rarely quick or easy. The Old Testament prophet **Habakkuk** teaches us that leaders must learn to cherish the time of waiting before they receive their answers. In Chapter One, the prophet is positioned to watch and see. In Chapter Two, he is positioned to stand and see. In Chapter Three, he is positioned to kneel and see. God declares five "woes" to Habakkuk in the second chapter of his book, describing his intense displeasure with his people. Yet, if God is sovereign, reigning over everything, why doesn't He use His leader to bring about justice immediately? The answer is this: While Habakkuk waited, God did an excellent work in his heart. Before God leads the world, He first wants to lead his leaders. **Habakkuk** learned at least four lessons about God's leadership in the world. (1) Not everything that happens conforms to God's will and wishes. (2) Nothing that happens gets overlooked by God. (3) Everything that happens will ultimately be addressed with justice, and (4) Nothing that happens should distract us from continuing to respond faithfully. ***Adapted from John Maxwell Leadership Bible. A division of Thomas Nelson, Inc.***

To achieve your goals, take a moment to confidently address these three key questions: "What are my roles?" "What are my key relationships within each role?" and "What responsibilities come with each of those relationships?" This reflection will empower you to move forward with clarity and purpose.

4.6 Endurance

As with processing, every effective leader must undergo an endurance test. You could call this a wilderness experience or say it is a test of tenacity and faithfulness. The test will answer this question: when your back is up against the wall, will you quit or endure the hardship as a good soldier of the cross? Jesus provides our most visible example. We will discuss this in greater detail in a later chapter, but as Jesus was led into the wilderness by the Spirit to be tempted by the devil, so will we. In the wilderness, we are equipped with survival skills and the ability to thrive under pressure. The principle is this: leaders cannot take others where they have never been. The Joseph story recounted in the Old Testament book of **Genesis 37-50** provides an excellent case study.

Whether you are willing to admit it or not, everyone starts out with naivety. And that's precisely where we find Joseph as his story began. He had little understanding of family dynamics. Perhaps he could not imagine how his brothers felt when he described his magnificent dreams, or maybe he didn't care. The Scripture says his brothers already hated him because he was their father's favorite child. And when he described his dreams, they hated him even more. Joseph said and did things that proved he had no idea what it meant to be a successful leader, as his dreams stipulated. It's easy to see why successful leaders must be aware of the implications of their actions and words. For Joseph, the cost of his ignorance was catastrophic.

Joseph's life-transforming journey began when he was sold into slavery in Egypt. It was here that he started to learn things he'd never learned in his early childhood. In time, he realized that leadership was difficult and carried a huge weight of responsibility." Along the way, he was betrayed and learned hard lessons of human nature, relationships, and leadership. The process shaped his character, teaching him both patience and humility. Eventually, he recognized God as his source of blessing and power.

Leaders who show great skill when opportunities arise shine only because they have paid the price. When Pharaoh finally called Joseph, the young man performed with excellence and great wisdom. But we must understand that he didn't succeed because he suddenly got wise at age thirty; he succeeded because he paid the price for what must have seemed like an endless thirteen years. Joseph's hard-won wisdom and discernment earned him a promotion to second-in-command of what was then the most powerful nation on earth.

During seven years of plenty, Joseph executed his leadership strategy with great skill. He filled the cities of Egypt with grain and prepared the country for the time of famine. However, we only saw how much his leadership skills had matured by observing what he did during the lean years. While he focused on feeding the people of Egypt, the strength of his leadership enabled him to feed people in other lands as well. In the process, he brought untold financial wealth, livestock, and land into his country's coffers, fulfilling the prophetic dreams of his youth.

Joseph endured years of challenges, including hatred from his brothers, who sold him into slavery, false allegations, and incarceration. Had it not been for his God-given destiny and purpose, faithfulness, and good character, he could have died having not fulfilled his dreams. Becoming a spiritually dynamic leader is much like a long-term business investment. If you hope to make a fortune in the short term, you will be very disappointed; what you do daily over the long haul matters most. If you continually develop your leadership skills, the inevitable result will be growth toward success.

4.7 Effective Leadership is a Learnt Art

As previously mentioned, although some people are born with more extraordinary natural gifts than others, the good news is that all leadership skills can be learned and improved. The most crucial point to note is that the process will not necessarily happen overnight. Leadership has many facets, including, but not limited to, experience, emotional strength, people skills, discipline, vision, momentum, and timing. That's why leaders require so much preparation to be effective. The good news is that, regardless of your starting point, you can improve your ability to become a successful leader through practice.

It is obvious that in his formative years, Joseph was unfit to work with others. He lacked knowledge, wisdom, tact, and humility—all qualities of an effective spiritual leader that only come with time and experience. Joseph's life is an excellent example of the law of process. Time and experience were largely responsible for the development of his leadership skills.

Every effective leader needs time to develop, but time alone cannot make someone effective. Some individuals never discover the law of process, work at growth, and never get past the initial stage.

Fortunately for the children of Israel, Joseph did not stop at the first stage. He grew in his journey from the pit to the palace. Nearly twenty-three years had elapsed before he was reunited with his family. In becoming a good follower and then a leader, he was groomed for a much greater purpose than he ever imagined as a proud teenager.

By his father's death, Joseph had learned to see things from God's perspective. When his brothers feared for their lives, Joseph reassured them by saying, "Do not be afraid, for I am in the place of God. But as for you, you meant it for evil against me, but God meant it for good, to bring it about as it is this day, to save many people alive" (**Genesis 50: 19-20**). At last, Joseph could trace God's hand from beginning to fulfillment over the timeline of his life. At that point, he finally understood the wisdom of God's long-term plan to save His people during the famine, a strategy in which Joseph played a major role. The question I would like to ask you here is, have you endured, or are you prepared to endure the process?

Chapter Checklist

In Review

- Successful spiritual leadership takes sacrifice, processing, and endurance
- Put people first
- Emphasize honesty and integrity
- Encourage leaps of faith and innovation
- Embrace change

- Foster a learning environment

- Establish open communication

- Must go through processing for character building and reshaping

- Must have a spirit of discernment

- Must learn to take responsibility

- Must have integrity

- Must be trustworthy

- Must have endurance

Personal Notes

_____

_____

_____

_____

_____

_____

_____

SECTION TWO

HOW TO RAISE SUCCESSFUL LEADERS

CHAPTERS 5 – 6

WHAT YOU NEED TO EMBODY IS ROOTED IN;

HOW LEADERS ARE CULTIVATED AND NU-TURED

Chapter Five
RAISING LEADERS (A HUMAN PERSPECTIVE)

For generations, both the secular society and the Church have adopted methods of raising leaders totally out of sync with God's pattern. It is common practice to bring people into leadership for the wrong reasons, with the wrong motives, and the wrong qualifications. This, however, is one of the most crucial aspects of effective leadership that should not be ignored.

If you are going to maximize your full leadership potential, one of the main criteria for success is rooted in the way you arrived at the place where you are holding that position of authority. In many cases, it only conforms to human tradition and values. Therefore, we must challenge the status quo and restore things to equilibrium with God's divine purpose and plan.

To restore balance within our organizations, we must undertake a comprehensive transformation of our mindsets and approaches to leader development. This shift involves a meticulous re-examination of our existing practices, critically analyzing what has and hasn't worked. It also calls for an open-minded embrace of innovative strategies that actively promote the growth of effective leaders, equipping them with the skills and insights necessary to navigate the complexities of today's challenges.

In this chapter, we will examine the criteria most organizations use to select and appoint leaders and compare them with God's criteria in the following chapter.

The following are examples of how modern organizations develop leaders and how some leaders attain their positions—the list is not exhaustive.

5.1 Academic Credentials

As I noted in chapter one, subsection three, earthly wisdom is not necessarily among God's criteria for leadership success. From a human perspective, however, academic credentials are probably the most critical benchmark for appointing leaders. In modern organizations, appointing individuals to leadership positions solely on the basis of academic achievement is standard practice, and the church is no exception. Although academic credentials are essential, they are not the most critical criterion God requires. You cannot find any such principles taught anywhere in the Bible. Please do not get me wrong; I am by no means underestimating the value of academic qualifications in these circumstances, and neither am I suggesting you should not seek to advance yourself academically. I would suggest that you take the initiative to ensure that you obtain the highest possible academic qualifications. However, while pursuing your academics, always remember that the world's accreditation process is much different from what God requires. **Proverbs 1:1-7** explains it like this:

> *"The proverbs of Solomon, the son of David, king of Israel: To know wisdom and instruction, To perceive the words of understanding, To receive the instruction of wisdom, Justice, judgment, and equity; To give prudence to the simple, To the young man knowledge and discretion—A wise man will hear and increase learning, And a man of understanding will attain wise counsel. To understand a proverb and an enigma, the word of the wise and their riddles. The fear of the Lord is the beginning of knowledge, but fools despise wisdom and instructions."*

In addition, **Luke 10:21** tells us that what is hidden from the wise and prudent is revealed to babes and suckling. In essence, the fear of the Lord is of far greater significance than any other source when it comes to obtaining knowledge.

To support my point, every year, hundreds of thousands of people enter theological and other educational institutions to pursue their aspirations to become successful spiritual leaders; yet, as noted earlier, statistics indicate that the vast majority fail to attain leadership positions.

So what is the problem? Some requirements cannot be taught in seminaries. For example, the fear of the Lord, experience, and particularly a "wilderness experience" (the process), is a far more extraordinary source of obtaining the wisdom of God, as nothing else can. I am sure you have heard the old dictum, "Experience is the route through which knowledge is gained."

> "Experience is the route through which knowledge is gained"

Let me emphasize again that this is not intended to undermine the value of education or the significant role educational institutions play in our society. I am truly proud of my accomplishments, particularly my journey through higher education, which includes earning a university degree and postgraduate studies. These experiences have played a vital role in shaping both my personal growth and my professional development. However, as we dive deeper into the essence of spiritual leadership, it becomes increasingly clear that genuine effectiveness in this role demands far more than mere academic qualifications. It requires a profound understanding of human connection, compassion, and the capacity to inspire others, which cannot be achieved solely through formal education. Becoming a dynamic and impactful spiritual leader requires a deep understanding of human experience, empathy, and the capacity to inspire and connect with others at every level.

5.2 Oratorical Skills

During my years of association with the church, I have seen many people appointed to leadership roles, not because they possessed strong leadership skills or were even solidly grounded spiritually. Many are appointed because of their rhetorical skills. Once again, I am not implying anything wrong with having excellent oratory skills; it's a great gift. However, please note that eloquence of speech is distinct from effective communication, which is vital for a leader.

The tragedy is that these mistakes are being repeated from one generation to the next and are responsible for many of the problems in the Body of Christ today. Being highly educated and able to speak eloquently does not guarantee you will make an excellent spiritual leader. And there can be no better role model for communication than Christ Himself. Jesus communicated simply and so effectively that everyone could understand, except, of course, for parables, some of which are spiritually discerned.

5.3 Force

Some leaders assume leadership by force. By this, I mean people who either position themselves as leaders (self-imposed leaders) or pressure themselves into leadership roles previously held by others. For instance, you may have heard the term "military coup." This is where the military overthrows a government and seizes power by force. This principle also applies when an influential church member, such as a deacon or a lay minister, splits the church to start his ministry. The harsh reality is that any leader who assumes leadership by force is destined for failure in the long run. Before you protest, let me explain. The Bible has much to say, and forced takeovers are not part of God's plan. To take a leadership position by force, you would have to push the current leader out of the role or split the organization and take part of his followers with you.

Here is what **Romans 13 1-2** says on the subject. "Let every soul be subject to the governing authorities. There is no authority except from God, and God appoints the existing authorities. Therefore, whoever resists the authority resists the ordinance of God, and those who resist will bring judgment on themselves."

Notice that the Bible says every authority is from God and that there are consequences for resisting God's authority. Having said this, although obedience to earthly authority is a general rule, you must disobey if commanded to sin. In essence, obedience to God always takes precedence over all human authority (**Esther 4:16, Daniel 3:12-18, 6:10, Matthew 2:12; Acts 5:29; Hebrews 11:23**). **Romans 13** went on to say;

> *"For a ruler is not a terror to good works, but to evil. Do you want to be unafraid of the authority? Do what is good, and you will have praise from the same. For he is God's minister to you for good. But if you do evil, be afraid; for he does not bear the sword in vain; for he is God's minister, an avenger to execute wrath on him who practices evil. Therefore, you must be subject, not only because of wrath but also for conscience's sake. For this reason, you also pay taxes, for they are God's ministers attending continually to this very thing. Render therefore to all their due: taxes to whom taxes custom to whom customs, fear to whom fear, honor to whom honor."*

In essence, the grace of God, accompanied by the teachings of the gospel of Christ, encourages us to adopt a posture of submission, even when our natural instincts might urge us to complain or feel bitter.

This principle reminds us that, regardless of our personal opinions about those in positions of authority, we are to honor and obey them, as their power is derived from God Himself. Having said that, please note that this submission is based on the understanding that it does not lead us into wrongdoing or sin. In other words, under no circumstances should you submit yourself to those who do not submit to the principles of Christ.

Additionally, I am acutely aware of the complexities this teaching presents. There are instances in which certain leaders may misinterpret their authority, perceiving it as a license to manipulate or exploit those under their care. This potential for misuse highlights the need for discernment and accountability within leadership. In the general course of human life, rulers are not a terror to people who live honestly and with integrity, but governmental authorities do strike terror in the hearts of transgressors. Such is the power of sin and corruption. Many will be kept from committing crimes only out of fear of punishment. **1 Timothy 2:1-3** says: "Therefore I exhort first of all that supplications, prayers, intercessions, *and* giving of thanks be made for all men, for kings and all who are in authority, that we may lead a quiet and peaceable life in all godliness and reverence. For this *is* good and acceptable in the sight of God our Savior." In other words, we should pray for those in authority and not resort to deception or fraud for selfish ends. Thus, the Bible says that rebellion goes against God's express command. It is not acceptable for any minister of the gospel to use manipulation to gain any leadership position.

5.4 Self-acclaimed leadership

Self-acclaimed leaders set themselves up in leadership out of selfish ambition. They usually have no accountability and sometimes no confirmation of God's call to such a position. Here are some of the problems associated with such leaders. Some people assume leadership positions because they refuse to submit to those whom God has set in authority over them. And as you may already be well aware, to refuse to submit to authority, you have already failed because greatness comes through your willingness to serve others. In addition, you will likewise have problems getting others to submit to you. In other words, you'll reap what you sow. Unless you are certain that God has given you a clear mandate, validated by the testimony of two or more witnesses, assuming leadership on your own is unwise.

5.5 Personality

Then there are those who are appointed for their personalities. There can be no doubt about the importance of having a good personality if you are going to succeed in leadership. But once again, this cannot be your primary reason for appointing anyone to a position of spiritual leadership. Succeeding as a spiritual leader requires more than an excellent personality. When selecting people for leadership, you must remember that the church is not just another democratic, political, or business organization. The church is a heavenly kingdom organization led by Jesus Christ, who is recognized as the supreme ruler and head of the church. Therefore, His gifts (spiritual gifts) are required to be effective in His kingdom. **Ephesians 4:7-9** explains it like this;

Spiritual Gifts

"But to each one of us grace was given according to the measure of Christ's gift. Therefore, He says: "When He ascended on high, He led captivity captive, and gave gifts to men." (Now this, "He ascended"—what does it mean but that He also first descended into the lower parts of the earth? He who descended is also the One who ascended far above all the heavens, that He might fill all things.) And He Himself gave some to be apostles, some prophets, some evangelists, and some pastors and teachers, for the equipping of the saints for the work of ministry, for the edifying of the Body of Christ, till we all come to the unity of the faith and of the knowledge of the Son of God, to a perfect man, to the measure of the stature of the fullness of Christ; that we should no longer be children, tossed too and fro and carried about with every wind of doctrine, by the trickery of men, in the cunning craftiness of deceitful plotting, but, speaking the truth in love, may grow up in all things into Him who is the head—Christ—from whom the whole body, joined and knit together by what every joint supplies, according to the effective working by which every part does its share, causes growth of the body for the edifying of itself in love."

The New Man

"This I say, therefore, and testify in the Lord, that you should

no longer walk as the rest of the Gentiles walk, in the futility of their mind, having their understanding darkened, being alienated from the life of God, because of the ignorance that is in them, because of the blindness of their heart; who, being past feeling, have given themselves over to lewdness, to work all uncleanness with greediness. But you have not so learned Christ, if indeed you have heard Him and have been taught by Him, as the truth is in Jesus: that you put off, concerning your former conduct, the old man which grows corrupt according to the deceitful lusts, and be renewed in the spirit of your mind, ^{24} and that you put on the new man which was created according to God, in true righteousness and holiness."

Therefore, the spiritual leader must not only be a people person with a good personality but must also be regenerated, a possessor of the gift of Christ, walking in true righteousness and holiness, honest, creative, confident, driven, courageous, and, more importantly, in love with Christ.

5.6 Favoritism or Hereditary Means

How often have you come across leaders chosen through favoritism or heredity? Many are appointed to leadership positions simply because they were born into a particular family. For example, the son of a company CEO, the offspring of the bishop or pastor, or other connected persons, such as someone in whom the leader has a vested interest. It could be someone who brings something of great physical value to the organization, such as wealth. And although this may be acceptable in secular society, it should not be so in the Kingdom of God. Just because you are the son of a pastor does not automatically make you an heir to the throne. You must earn your place and be called by God for such an appointment. If you are appointed by heredity, it means you could be assigned to a position for which you do not have the gift and calling of God. The long-term implications of this could be catastrophic. It's no wonder there are so many people in positions of influence with no real heart for the work and very little impact on the lives of their followers. Do you remember the story in **Genesis 49** when Jacob assembled his sons for a time of impartation and blessing at the end of his life? By heredity, Reuben should have assumed the leadership of his family, but disqualified himself through his actions. Once he was disqualified, the next in line should have taken his place, but both the second and third (Simeon and Levi) were disqualified as well.

"And Jacob called his sons and said, Gather together, that I may tell you what shall befall you in the last days: Gather together and hear, you sons of Jacob, and listen to Israel your father. Reuben, you are my firstborn, my might and the beginning of my strength, the excellency of dignity and the excellency of power. Unstable as water, you shall not excel, because you went up to your father's bed; then you defiled it—He went up to my couch. Simeon and Levi are brothers; instruments of cruelty are in their dwelling place. Let not my soul enter their council; Let not my honor be united to their assembly; for in their anger they slew a man, and in their self-will, they hamstrung an ox. Cursed be their anger, for it is fierce; And their wrath, for it is cruel! I will divide them

*in Jacob. And scatter them in Israel" **(Genesis 49:1-7)**.*

So we see here then that Reuben was disqualified, described as unstable as water. Instability often disqualifies otherwise gifted people from becoming effective leaders. **James 1:8** says that a double-minded person is unstable in not some but all of his/her ways. You see the importance of being "steadfast, immovable, always abounding in the works of the Lord." The other two brothers were disregarded because of their cruelty to both man and animal—unreliable or compassionate. But now let's look at the person Jacob saw fit to appoint to a leadership role. **Genesis 49:8-10**:

> *"Judah, you are he whom your brothers shall praise; your hand shall be on the neck of your enemies; your father's children shall bow down before you. Judah is a lion's whelp; from the prey, my son, you have gone up. He bows down; he lies down as a lion, and as a lion, who shall rouse him? The scepter shall not depart from Judah, nor a lawgiver from between his feet, until Shiloh comes; and to him shall be the obedience of the people."*

Judah means "praise"; therefore, Jacob acknowledged that a life of praise will always draw God's presence. If you are a worshipper, you will be respected and honored, vital attributes of spiritual leadership. "It is you whom your brothers will praise." This passage also applies to us as believers; it is you whom your followers will praise. Also, "your hand shall be in the neck of your enemy." In other words, your praise shall choke the enemy to death. Then Jacob concluded by saying, "The scepter shall not depart from Judah, nor a law given from beneath his feet." The scepter represents authority and power. This means that power and authority shall not depart from those who fear and worship God. This is powerful stuff; in the end, you will see that a lifestyle of praise and worship is pivotal to a leader's success.

Notice that raising leaders from a human perspective does not take into consideration some critical spiritual factors, as follows:

- It does not consider the individual's spiritual maturity, integrity, and commitment.

- It does not consider whether the person knows the way through the wilderness—and once again, you know what the Bible says will happen if the blind leads the blind—yes, they both will fall into the ditch.

- It does not take into consideration whether or not the leader has a vision, and

- It does not consider whether the leader understands his or her purpose.

Do you remember when Israel decided they wanted a king (a physical, earthly leader)? This was the exact mistake they made. Their choice was Saul; he encapsulated many of these human attributes. The Bible explains, "There was not a more handsome person than he among the children of Israel, from his shoulders upward he was taller than any of the people" **1 Samuel 9:2.** Notice that the Bible is describing the people's choice, and the emphasis of the people's choice is his physical attributes. Even the instrument of his anointing ceremony was man-made; the Bible says Samuel took a flask of oil… 1 Samuel 2:1 (the flask was a man-made instrument), but not so when it came to God's choice.

When God wanted to choose a king, he chose the opposite of man's choice, David. His physical stature stood in stark contrast to Saul's. We are not told that he was trained in the military forces, as his brothers were, nor that he was in line for such a position, as custom and family tradition of his day dictated.

We will discuss this in greater detail in the following chapter, but in **1 Samuel 16:13,** "Then Samuel took a horn of oil and anointed him among his brothers and the Spirit of the Lord came upon David from that day forward… A horn is a God-made instrument.

In reality, the human perspective is geared towards giving people positions to entice them to be faithful and triumphant in their organization—but they could not be more wrong about this approach.

I am sorry to disappoint some of you, but as I have said several times before and will say here again, the measure of your success is not dependent solely upon your charisma, academia, eloquence, affluence, social status, or even your outward appearance. While these characteristics are essential, achieving excellence depends on your ability to recognize problems and devise viable solutions.

Make no mistake about it: if you did not arrive at the leadership position the way God intended, your reign could be short-lived, as Saul's was.

In the next chapter, we will examine the attributes of God's choice in appointing a leader.

Chapter Checklist

In Review

- It is standard practice to bring people to the position of leadership for the wrong reasons, wrong motives, and the wrong qualifications.

- Everyone is a potential leader, and because God has called you to such a position, your success is guaranteed

- If you have not arrived where you're holding your leadership position as God intended, your reign may be short-lived.

- Here is a list of human criteria for the appointment of leaders:

    - Academic credentials.

    - Oratorical skills.

    - Personality.

    - By force.

    - Self-acclaim leadership.

    - By favoritism and hereditary means.

It is important to note that these do not consider any spiritual attributes, such as integrity, commitment, or wilderness experience. Additionally, it does not take into account whether the person has a vision or understands their purpose.

Personal Notes

Chapter Six
GOD'S PATTERN FOR RAISING LEADERS

In the previous chapter, we examined how leaders are developed from a human perspective. In this chapter, we will compare God's standard for raising leaders with that of the world.

As Chapter Five mentions, while attributes like academic credentials, public speaking skills, and charisma are important for effective leadership, they are not necessarily God's criteria for success. God can elevate individuals to leadership positions regardless of whether they hold a university degree, a master's degree, or even a doctorate. You may never have completed a leadership course or been a professional or celebrity. God rarely seeks out the most talented, gifted, or popular. He often calls ordinary people from the lowest places and backgrounds to undertake remarkable endeavors.

God does not need human credentials because when He calls you, He equips, enables, and provides all that is necessary for the task. In reality, God takes great pleasure in raising people out of abject obscurity to a place of significance. He delights in turning the ordinary into the extraordinary and enabling them to do great exploits for His kingdom.

Once again, I must remind you that this does not negate the fact that you must take all necessary steps to advance your skills. You should "be diligent to present yourself approved to God, a worker who does not need to be ashamed, rightly dividing the Word of truth" (**2 Timothy 2:15**). Every leader should be a student of the Word throughout his life. This means you need to aim high—remember, the sky is the limit to what you can achieve, and a good education is a good starting point.

So how does God call and raise leaders, and what credentials does God regard as necessary for the potential leader? One of the best ways to illustrate this point is to look at a couple of examples. In this regard, I cannot think of anyone more suitable than Moses, Israel's most outstanding leader, and David—the greatest king who ever lived. The lives of these men provide excellent case studies regarding how God raises leaders—let's look at them in turn.

6.1 Moses

Exodus 2 recounts one of the most remarkable calls of God and the rise to prominence of a leader. Moses was called from his lowly and undistinguished background of herding sheep to deliver from oppression, unquestionably one of the most extraordinary emancipations recorded in human history. I know you may want to challenge me on this, as Moses was brought up as a prince and highly educated in all the scientific knowledge of Egypt (**Act 7:22**). However, please note that at the time of his call by God, Moses was about eighty years old and had spent the last forty of those years in the desert as a servant to Jethro whose job was taking care of sheep. Before God could use him, you might say he was sent by God to the wilderness for forty years to rid him of his forty years of Egyptian pride, affluence, and influence. By this time, Moses had been brought down to earth; he did not even consider himself capable of speaking persuasively—neither did he boast of his royal upbringing or his educational opportunities.

The fact is that Moses was called by God long before he was appointed leader. The hand of God was clearly upon his life from birth; note the following scenes from his life.

When Moses was born, as **Exodus 2:2** recounts, his mother saw that he was a "proper child" meaning there was something special about him; she could see he had great potential. This is the reason she hid him for three months to escape the genocide for which Pharaoh was responsible for wiping out the Hebrew nation. When she could not hide him any longer, she made him "an ark of bulrushes." She set him aside and then had her daughter, Miriam, keep an eye on the ark. God planned for the daughter of Pharaoh to adopt the child. In a seemingly strange turn of events, his sister arranged for the child's mother to become his caretaker and be paid for the privilege. What an awesome God we serve!

You, too, when you were born, someone saw that you were a proper child with great potential. In addition, God specially designed you to accomplish great things in the kingdom. In the sight of God, you possess unique gifts and talents that only God knows. This is why you have been specially selected for the Master's purpose, a testament to your unique capabilities and strengths. If God has chosen you, it is because He has intricately fashioned you with everything required to achieve remarkable success. You could say that you are destined for greatness, equipped with the potential to rise above challenges and make a significant impact.

The first phase of his transition could not be considered perfect by any stretch of the imagination; it even included murder. Regardless of his faulty start, God saw in him one of the greatest qualities of a successful leader. For example, he was resolute in standing up for justice. This is not necessarily one of the human accolades for leadership, as mentioned above, but for God, this is absolutely essential.

6.1.1 Moses—A Man of Justice

The critical thing to note here is that before God could use him to accomplish anything of great significance, especially from a spiritual perspective, the first step in the right direction was to deal with his identity issues.

Although Moses was brought up as an Egyptian, he quickly identified with the Hebrews. You, too, must first deal with your identity, mainly to whom you belong. You must be aware that you are interconnected to God, and for this reason, you are called to be of service to Him and His people. **Exodus 2:11-13** tells us the story:

One day, he went out to his people, and while observing their oppression, he saw an Egyptian beating a Hebrew. He looked around, and seeing no one, he killed the Egyptian and buried him in the sand. When he went out the next day, he saw two Hebrews fighting, and he said to the one who was in the wrong, "Why do you strike your companion?" Notice the man's response to Moses—he questioned

Moses' authority and viewed him as a murderer. He answered, "Who made you a ruler and a judge over us? Do you mean to kill me as you killed the Egyptian?" "Then Moses was afraid and thought, surely the thing is known." When Pharaoh heard it, he sought to kill Moses.

Before God could use him, you might say he was sent by God to the wilderness for forty years to rid him of his forty years of Egyptian pride, affluence, and influence.

6.1.2 Moses—as a Type of Savior

In the next scene from his adult life, we find him on the run. He came to Median to hide, and Moses witnessed yet another act of oppression as he sat on a well. The shepherds drove away the seven daughters of the priest of Median, preventing them from watering their animals. This time, he is a savior and draws water for the women. **Exodus 2:15-21** tells the whole story:

> *"But Moses fled from Pharaoh. He settled in the land of Median and sat down by a well. The priest of Median had seven daughters. They came to draw water and fill the troughs to water their father's flock. But some shepherds came and drove them away. Moses got up and came to their defense and watered the flock. When they returned to their father, Reuel, (Jethro) he said 'How is it that you have come back so soon today?' They said, 'An Egyptian helped us against the shepherds; he even drew water for us and watered the flock.' He said to his daughters, 'Where is he? Why did you leave the man? Invite him to break bread.'*

> *Moses agreed to stay with the man, and in the end he gave Moses his daughter Zipporah in marriage."*

Before God elevates someone to a leadership position, He meticulously prepares them long before the responsibility is entrusted to them. This was evident in the life of Moses, whose journey was marked by various experiences that shaped his character and resolve. Through trials and challenges, God was actively equipping Moses for a monumental task: to lead His people out of the shackles of slavery. Each moment in Moses's life served a purpose, honing his skills and strengthening his faith, ensuring he was ready to fulfill the divine mission that lay ahead.

As I have said before, you cannot take anyone where you have never been. In other words, you cannot effectively and confidently take others to their destination unless you know where you are going and how to get there. In the first instance, Moses was classified as a murderer, but on this occasion, he acted as a type of savior, which was to be his destiny: to deliver the children of Israel from bondage.

6.1.3 Moses—A Committed Servant

Another vitally important leadership characteristic Moses possessed was his willingness and commitment to serve: "Now Moses was tending the flock of Jethro, his father-in-law, the priest of Median. And he led the flock to the back of the desert, and came to Horeb, the mountain of God." Notice something here; the Bible says that Moses led the sheep into the backside of the desert.

One translation says "deep *into the backside of the desert."* Friends, that's what I call dedication. In my opinion, the ultimate test of commitment is to show this kind of dedication when carrying out a task considered menial and unimportant, especially when no one is watching you. Yes, we like to display our gifts and talents in the spotlight, but we can sometimes adopt a "don't care" attitude when no one is looking.

> This is what the Apostle meant when he said, "Be obedient to those who are your masters according to the flesh, with fear and trembling, in sincerity of heart, as to Christ; not with eye service, as men-pleasers, but as bondservants of Christ, doing the will of God from the heart" (**Ephesians 6:5-6**).

To illustrate, if you want to become a successful leader, a commitment to every task, no matter how insignificant it may seem, is critical. Every task offers a valuable opportunity for personal growth and allows God to develop your humility. Embracing these moments can revolutionize and strengthen your leadership qualities. Moses's intended destination was not originally the mountain of God; rather, it was his commitment to find new pastures for his sheep that brought him there. This shows that commitment can lead you to remarkable places and even to extraordinary encounters with God. The Bible says, "And the Angel of the Lord appeared to him in a flame of fire from the midst of a bush. So he looked, and behold, the bush was burning with fire, but the bush *was not* consumed. Then Moses said, "I will now turn aside and see this great sight, why the bush does not burn." It is noteworthy that Moses decided to turn aside. If you are going to become a spiritually effective leader, you must also set aside the ordinary activities of life so that God can get your attention. Notice that it was precisely at this moment that God seized His focus.

"Be obedient to those who are your masters according to the flesh, with fear and trembling, in the sincerity of heart, as to Christ; not with eye service, as men-pleasers, but as bondservants of Christ, doing the will of God from the heart"

"So when the Lord saw that he turned aside to look, God called to him from the midst of the bush and said, "Moses, Moses!" And he said, "Here I am." Then He said, "Do not draw near this place. Take your sandals off your feet, for the place where you stand is holy ground." Moreover, He said, "I am the God of your father—the God of Abraham, the God of Isaac, and the God of Jacob." And Moses hid his face, for he was afraid to look upon God. And the Lord said: "I have surely seen the oppression of My people who are in Egypt, and have heard their cry because of their taskmasters, for I know their sorrows. So I have come down to deliver them out of the hand of the Egyptians, and to bring them up from that land to a good and large land, to a land flowing with milk and honey, to the place of the Canaanites and the Hittites and the Amorites and the Perizzites and the Hivites and the Jebusites. Now therefore, behold, the cry of the children of Israel has come to Me, and I have also seen the oppression with which the Egyptians oppress them. Come now, therefore, and I will send you to Pharaoh that you may bring My people, the children of Israel, out of Egypt." But Moses said to God, "Who am I that I should go to Pharaoh, and that I should bring the children of Israel out of Egypt?" So He said, "I will certainly be with you. And this shall be a

sign to you that I have sent you: When you have brought the people out of Egypt, you shall serve God on this mountain" **(Exodus 3:1-12).**

As previously discussed, Moses and the Apostle Paul stand out as two of the most educated figures chosen by God to lead His people, setting them apart from many of their contemporaries. Moses received a rigorous education steeped in the scientific knowledge and rich traditions of ancient Egypt, a privilege that equipped him with a profound understanding of the natural world and governance. On the other hand, Paul had the distinguished honor of studying under Gamaliel, a revered scholar whose teachings were regarded as the pinnacle of academic excellence, akin to those of today's most prestigious universities, such as Oxford and Harvard.

Despite their impressive educational backgrounds, it is crucial to highlight that Moses' divine calling was not a result of his extensive learning. When God summoned him to undertake the monumental task of leading the Israelites out of slavery, Moses humbly questioned his own worthiness with the poignant words, "Who am I?" This sentiment mirrors the feelings expressed by Paul in his letter to the Corinthians **(1 Corinthians 2:1-5)**;

> *And I, brethren, when I came to you, did not come with excellence of speech or of wisdom declaring to you the testimony of God. For I determined not to know anything among you except Jesus Christ and Him crucified. I was with you in weakness, in fear, and in much trembling. And my speech and my preaching were not with persuasive words of human*

> *wisdom, but in demonstration of the Spirit and of power that your faith should not be in the wisdom of men but in the power of God.*

Here, Paul emphasizes his reliance on God's power rather than his abilities. As John Maxwell once said, "People don't care how much you know until they know how much you care." Moses cared for and hated injustice, especially concerning the people of God. The bottom line is that God raises leaders who honor Him, serve others, and care for those they lead and those with whom they come in contact in everyday life. God often gives the true leader the enthusiasm and self-assurance to face tough challenges. Once again, I understand that you may want to challenge me on this point, especially since Moses made not one but five excuses for not being up to the task of leading the children of Israel. But as I have said before, Moses was committed to the idea of freeing the Hebrew children from bondage long before God called him to the position. In the long run, leadership has little to do with man's opinions one way or the other.

6.2 David

Let's now focus on the extraordinary rise to prominence of unquestionably the greatest king that ever lived.

In chapter five, subsection six, I have cited David; "man after God's own heart" as God's choice as opposed to Saul, man's choice as king of Israel. There can be no more extraordinary Old Testament model for God's choice of a leader than David. **1 Samuel 16** tells us that God rejected Saul, "the people's choice" as king of Israel, and sent the prophet Samuel down to Jesse to anoint one of his sons, "God's choice." Samuel arrived at Jesse's home, having extended an invitation to the elders of Israel to join the sons of Jesse for an anointing service. The most significant observation here is that David was not even considered for an invitation to what would become his own anointing service.

So what do you think was the reason for this? The primary reason was that he was not considered qualified for the position. Some of you would immediately throw a tantrum if your leader did not call and present you to their congregation in an an elaborate anointing service to reinforce your sense of importance. But man's invitation is not necessarily God's choice. As I have said on occasion, a position based on man's ideal is insignificant as far as God is concerned. You may be sitting in the back of your thirty-thousand-seater church auditorium, and nobody ever notices you coming and going. Perhaps you are in a small village church on the other side of the world with very little hope of ever getting into the spotlight.

No one ever announced you as an anointed and dedicated servant of God, and to make matters worse, you have bought into the notion that there is no way you can ever be noticed. But, I must emphasize that it does not matter where you are right now—God is not looking for those in the limelight; He is looking for people with a servant's heart and a teachable spirit. He's looking for you; when appointed, He will raise you up, and many will be astounded by your extraordinary accomplishments.

> Some of you would immediately throw a tantrum if your pastor did not call you and present you to their congregation in an elaborate anointing service to reinforce your sense of importance.

Some of you would immediately throw a tantrum if your pastor did not call you and present you to their congregation in an elaborate anointing service to reinforce your sense of importance.

Because he was good-looking and strong, and according to tradition, Eliab, the eldest son, would have been Samuel's personal choice for leadership. But in verse 7, we read: "But the Lord said to Samuel, 'Do not look on his appearance, or the height of his stature, because I have rejected him; for the Lord does not see as mortals see; they look on the outward appearance, but the Lord looks at the heart.'" Jesse allowed seven of his sons to pass by Samuel in like manner, but Samuel said to Jesse each time, "The Lord has not chosen this one." Then, in (**1 Samuel 16:11**) "Samuel said to Jesse, are all your sons here?" and he said, "There remains yet the youngest, but he is keeping the sheep." Again, notice that Jesse tries to explain why he doesn't consider David qualified. He was the youngest and only a sheep boy. The remarkable truth is, it does not matter the position you hold currently or your present location—provided you possess the heart God is looking for, He will come and get you at the appointed time and raise you up from your lowly state to a place of prominence.

"And Samuel said to Jesse, 'Send and bring him, for we will not sit down until he comes here." Verse 12 went on to say: "So he sent and brought him in, now he was ruddy and had beautiful eyes, and handsome." It is said that David was a whole day's journey away (eleven miles being referred to in scripture as one day's journey); therefore, I must emphasize once again, you can rest assured that it doesn't matter where you are when God is ready to raise you up—nothing and no one can stand in your way.

6.2.1 David—Heart of a Servant

Perhaps you may be asking the question, what then qualified David as God's choice? He was a divinely chosen and charismatic leader, but it was clearly against tradition and protocol for the youngest son to be selected as the leader in his day and culture. Yet God's sovereign choice overrules human tradition in choosing a leader.

Notice that the Bible says nothing about David being an Eton Schoolboy or an Oxford, Cambridge, or Harvard University graduate type of education. We do know that, like Moses, he was a committed servant. So, how do I know this? Notice in **1 Samuel 17:34-37** David's response when Israel was confronted by the Philistine army, particularly the Philistine giant Goliath. The little fellow brought lunch for his brothers, and you know the story—he decided to go and fight the giant. His brothers and Saul tried to discourage him, but notice the act of defiance and commitment displayed by David in these statements:

> *But David said to Saul, "Your servant used to keep his father's sheep, and when a lion or a bear came and took a lamb out of the flock, I went out after it and struck it, and delivered the lamb from its mouth, and when it arose against me, I caught it by its beard, and struck and killed it. Your servant has killed both lion and bear; and this uncircumcised Philistine will be like one of them, seeing he has defied the armies of the living God." Moreover, David said, "The Lord, who delivered me from the paw of the lion and the paw of the bear, will deliver me from the hand of*

this Philistine."

Once again, it's not just what you do when you are in the spotlight; it's also what you do when no one is watching. Imagine facing a lion and a bear with your bare hands, especially when tasked with the most menial and humble duties. Under those circumstances, most of us would likely run away at the sight of a bear or a lion. Moses and David each honed their most admirable qualities away from the public eye, embracing a life of humility and solitude. In those quiet moments, with only God as their witness, they developed their characters and forged their destinies. This serves as a reminder: you, too, can nurture your inner strengths in the stillness, focusing on growth rather than the world's applause.

6.3 Affirmation and Mentoring

God will never raise up a leader unless He has confirmed him or her. "Through the mouths of one or two witnesses, the word shall be established" **(2 Corinthians 13:1).** When Moses told his father-in-law, Jethro, about his encounter at the burning bush, Jethro affirmed him. (See **Exodus 18:9-11**)

It would be best if you never ended up leading unless you have been mentored and have someone to whom you are accountable—personal accountability is a vital part of effective leadership. This is why I believe that after his anointing, God would have David, the young king, sent to Saul in waiting. You may assume it was to play comforting music for Saul in times of distress, but the primary purpose was to provide David with valuable royal training and development. This is why you must be prudent when it comes to those who have broken away from leadership and want to become independent, having received no form of mentoring and no spiritual covering. Once again, I must emphasize that I am not saying that everyone who has stepped away from a leader is out of order, because that may be warranted. The thing is, how these events are masterminded is of great importance. As mentioned earlier in **Romans 13:2-7**, submission to God-given authorities should not be taken lightly.

As Paul challenged the Romans, so he challenges us today; we, too, are to submit to God-given authorities. This means that every child should submit to their parents; every person should be subject to governments; every employee to their employers or managers; and most importantly, every child of God must be submitted to God and those in authority. God has not commanded this simply because leaders are always more competent and more reliable than the rest of you, not at all. God is providing us with an authority test. Before we can become leaders of integrity, we must learn to submit to those who lead us. This is true regardless of whether we think we are more capable, have a better approach to how things should be done, or are more educated and have better administrative skills. John Maxwell once said, "The acid test of character comes when we disagree with legitimate authorities; if we refuse to demand our way and instead submit to others, our hearts are right; this is when God can trust us to lead others." The obvious question is: if you are aspiring to become an effective leader, what motivates you, and what qualities are you bringing to the table? In other words, why do you believe you qualify? As I have said on previous occasions and will say again, it should never be because you have a long list of academic achievements after your name or because you can speak well. Once again, education, intelligence, and the gift of speaking with eloquence are vital attributes of an effective leader. However, according to the Word of God, this is not what God seeks. When God is raising a leader, He will build on the individual's strengths, experience, background, and heart. And further develop those kinds of skills over time. God used everything Moses possessed: his education, his knowledge of Pharaoh's operations, and his knowledge of Egypt's administration. Perhaps more importantly, he spent forty years on the backside of the desert. How does your experience compare to that? What do you possess that God can use? How much "real training" do you have? Real training here refers to character refinement, often in challenging circumstances.

Not long ago, the Holy Spirit spoke this revelation into my spirit: Son, when you are looking for someone to appoint to a position of leadership, look for those who are willing to serve. Not people from a particular social class, or the affluent, etc." The person who is willing to sweep the floor without being prompted is a great leader.

I am aware that all this is designed to challenge your thinking, and many of you will have to admit that this was not how you were anointed and appointed to leadership. Your tradition may have been to appoint people based on credentials and accolades. That may be one reason you are having difficulty achieving success in your ministry. In addition, it may also be one of the reasons the Holy Spirit has long departed—too much human input. Perhaps you're saying, "Well, Mr. Kerr, you just described exactly how I was brought to leadership and how I have chosen leaders to date. The question is, what should I do now?" Here are my suggestions:

I do not recommend the practice of demoting individuals, as it may necessitate a reassessment of your own position. Instead, I propose the following course of action:

Change your Mindset

- The first step in your journey toward effective leadership is to release the notion that true leaders are solely defined by their accomplishments and accolades. Instead, explore the myriad qualities and experiences that contribute to genuine leadership, focusing on attributes such as empathy, resilience, and vision. Embrace the idea that leadership can come from various backgrounds and must be nurtured through continuous learning and growth.

- **Look for those who are willing to serve**

Look at your congregation and note those willing to serve, especially regarding the most menial tasks.

Yes, I do mean that—people who are faithful in little will accomplish much. A good prospective leader should be willing to start at the bottom, not at the top.

> When you're looking to appoint someone to a leadership position, look for those willing to serve.

When you're looking for someone to appoint to a leadership position, look for those willing to serve.

Zachariah 4:10 "Do not despise the day of small beginnings" (NLT)

Can you recall how Jesus demonstrated this? He did so by washing the disciples' feet. God promised to acknowledge this by saying, "Well done, thou good and faithful servant," Not well done, thou gifted, powerful, and anointed one.

Servanthood is paramount when bringing someone to prominence in leadership for several reasons. Here are a few such reasons;

6.4 Stability

Stability in leadership hinges on the character and integrity of those in charge. As an illustration, let's return to Jacob's leadership appointment, as mentioned earlier in chapter 5, subsection 6, **"Favoritism and Hereditary Means."** The appointment of a Leader such as Reuben, whose moral failings were evident, often undermines the stability of their leadership. By prioritizing leaders with strong ethical foundations, as Jacob did with Judah, we can ensure a stable and trustworthy leadership. Stable leadership requires wise decision-making. Jacob's choice to bypass Reuben in favor of Judah exemplifies the importance of discerning leadership appointments. This ensures that leaders are not only spiritually qualified but also capable of fostering long-term stability and success within the organization or community. Stability is also deeply rooted in the trust between leaders and their followers. Reuben's actions damaged trust, whereas Judah eventually earned it.

Leaders who act transparently and reliably can build and maintain trust, which is essential for stability. Stable leadership looks beyond the present and focuses on building a legacy for future generations. Jacob's prophetic blessings were intended to ensure that the tribes of Israel would have a stable and prosperous future.

By applying these principles to the concept of stability, we can create leadership frameworks that are resilient, trustworthy, and forward-thinking. This not only strengthens the present leadership but also paves the way for a stable and prosperous future.

This serves as a profound reminder that when raising leaders, it is essential to align choices with God's intended pattern and purpose, prioritizing character over convention and capability above mere celebrity status.

6.5 Hard Work

In addition to stability, God's desire is for every successful leader to learn and appreciate the value of hard work. That's why it takes a person with a servant's heart to lead effectively. Occasionally, a physically challenging work application is required without earthly reward. In our case study, Moses first encountered God when he took his father-in-law's sheep <u>deep</u> into the back of the desert. Can you think of a more committed and determined servant than Moses? He was not in a meeting with the elders trying to impress upon them the need to review his credentials obtained in Egypt, nor was he trying to convince anyone. He was simply a hard worker committed to the task at hand, and in due time, God revealed Himself to him in a compelling object lesson. Notice that the same can be said of David. Hard work and determination led him to defend his sheep with everything he had, even if it meant using his bare hands and risking his life. There are some other instances in scripture where God raised leaders in this same manner.

It is every leader's responsibility to raise others who are capable of not only succeeding them, but also capable of running with the vision should they be unable to fulfill it.

For instance, God declared Jephthah as "a mighty man of valor," empowering him to rise up and rescue His people from the threats posed by the Ammonites. In a parallel situation, Gideon was greeted with the words, "The Lord is with you, you mighty man of valor." This powerful affirmation instilled courage in Gideon, who had been hesitant and afraid. Inspired by this divine encouragement, he found the strength to embrace his role as a leader and undertake the daunting challenge of liberating Israel from the oppressive Midianites. **Judges 6:11.**

6.6 Vision

As highlighted in chapter three, every effective leader possesses a compelling vision that fuels their actions, allowing them to patiently wait for the opportune moment to bring that vision to fruition in alignment with God's timing. Moses is a prime example of this kind of visionary leadership; he boldly stepped forward to defend his people long before he envisioned himself in a leadership role. His early acts of bravery demonstrated not only his commitment to his people but also his deep understanding of their struggles, laying the groundwork for the monumental journey that lay ahead. David also, in an act of defiance, defended his sheep long before he was anointed king and before he recognized the need to defend Israel in his capacity as leader. In addition to having a vision, God will always bring others to support leaders and compensate for any weaknesses they may have. That's why God gave Aaron to Moses as spokesman, Joshua as his army general, and Hur as a supporter in the battle. This is why Jonathan befriended

David when, in fact, he should have hated him, as David was taking Jonathan's rightful inheritance to the throne. No one can succeed without others supporting them. Put another way, it does not matter how naturally gifted you are or how much charisma you have; you need the support of others to help you get to your destination. This is one of the reasons it is every leader's responsibility to raise others who are capable not only of succeeding him but also of running with the vision should he be unable to fulfill it.

So, to summarize, what makes an excellent potential leader? Some people are naturally gifted to lead, and their leadership potential will be obvious. Others may not possess those natural gifts and qualities, but they are prepared to take initiative and work hard to develop their skills. One word of caution: we have to be careful because some can appear to be front-runners when all they want is to be seen as men—a situation to be avoided at all costs. As you can imagine, it will take prayer and discernment to determine the motives of such men, but God will deposit it in your spirit if He disapproves. A true leader embodies humility and dedication, readily embracing any task without needing applause or acknowledgment. These individuals often shine as servant leaders, prioritizing the needs of others above their own. This selfless approach is a crucial indicator of their potential to become outstanding spiritual leaders, guiding others with compassion and purpose.

In the previous two chapters, we delved into the contrasting paths of leadership development, focusing on how leaders are usually selected and appointed in everyday life. In stark contrast, we also examined how God chooses and raises leaders for His purposes. By doing so, we strive to illuminate the unique leadership styles of humanity and divinity, thereby deepening our understanding and inspiring more effective leadership practices.

In the chapters to come, we will take a closer look at specific biblical models that exemplify these differences, illuminating the distinct approaches of human methodologies compared to the divine wisdom of God's ways.

Chapter Preview

In Review

- God raises leaders by His own sovereign will.

- God raises leaders regardless of whether that person has a university degree, completed a leadership course, is a professional, has a master's degree, or has a doctorate degree.

- When God calls you, He equips, enables, and provides all the necessary tools for the task.

- While you should seek to attain the highest level of education, it is not necessarily God's criteria.

- God will always give a true leader a feeling of enthusiasm and self-assurance to face the challenges of leadership.

- God will never raise a leader unless He has affirmed him/her.

- No one should end up in a leadership role without having some form of mentoring.

- Paul challenges us to submit to God-given authority.

- You must be aware of your motivation when considering a position of authority.

- When you are looking for someone to be promoted to a leadership position, look for those who are willing to serve.

- Stability is crucial for leadership success.

- Every successful leader must have an appreciation for the value of hard work.

Personal Notes

SECTION THREE

BIBLICAL MODELS OF

LEADERSHIP
- ✓ Inspire People
- ✓ Empower People
- ✓ Shared Vision
- ✓ Lead Change

CHAPTERS 7 – 8

TO MAKE IT TO THE TOP;

YOU MUST START AT THE BOTTOM

Chapter Seven
Old Testament Model of Leadership

In the archives of ancient scriptures, the Old Testament stands as a testament to the enduring principles of divine leadership. From the deserts of Egypt to the palaces of Israel, the Old Testament presents a vivid tapestry of leaders whose lives were shaped by their unwavering faith and obedience to God. These leaders, flawed yet faithful, offer timeless lessons on the essence of true leadership. I would like to invite you to join me on an extraordinary journey through the sands of time as we explore the life of Joshua, a remarkable biblical model of leadership. Together, we will uncover the wisdom and virtues that made him an inspiring figure, one who continues to guide us today.

Before we embark on Joshua's inspiring leadership journey, it is beneficial first to recognize the key qualities that characterize biblical leadership. Understanding these qualities will not only illuminate Joshua's path but also provide valuable insights for today's leaders. Biblical leadership qualities are based on principles and characteristics exemplified by many leaders in the Bible. Let's explore some of these fundamental qualities:

1. **Humility**: Leaders such as Moses and Jesus, among others, demonstrated humility. They served others selflessly, putting the needs of their people above their own (**Philippians 2:3-8**). ³ "*Let* nothing *be done* through selfish ambition or conceit, but in lowliness of mind let each esteem others better than himself. ⁴ Let each of you look out not only for his own interests but also for the interests of others. Let this mind be in you which was also in Christ Jesus, ⁶ who, being in the form of God, did not consider it [b]robbery to be equal with God, ⁷ but [c]made Himself of no reputation, taking the form of a bondservant, *and* coming in the likeness of men. ⁸ And being found in appearance as a man, He humbled Himself and became obedient to *the point of* death, even the death of the cross"

2. **Integrity:** Biblical leaders uphold integrity, maintaining strong moral and ethical principles. Job is often highlighted for his unwavering integrity (Job 27:5-6). "Far be it from me that I should say you are right; Till I die, I will not put away my integrity from me. ⁶ The righteousness I hold fast and will not let it go; My heart shall not reproach *me* as long as I live."

3. **Servant Leadership:** Jesus taught and exemplified servant leadership, emphasizing serving others over seeking power (Mark 10:42-45). "⁴² But Jesus called them to *Himself* and said to them, "You know that those who are considered rulers over the Gentiles lord it over them, and their great ones exercise authority over them. ⁴³ Yet it shall not be so among you; but

whoever desires to become great among you shall be your servant. **⁴⁴** And whoever of you desires to be first shall be slave of all. **⁴⁵** For even the Son of Man did not come to be served, but to serve, and to give His life a ransom for many."

4. **Wisdom**: Leaders such as Solomon asked God for wisdom to govern effectively, showing that wise decision-making is crucial (1 Kings 3:9-12). **⁹** Therefore, give to Your servant an understanding heart to judge Your people, that I may discern between good and evil. For who is able to judge these great people of Yours?" **¹⁰** The speech pleased the Lord, that Solomon had asked this thing. **¹¹** Then God said to him: "Because you have asked this thing, and have not asked long life for yourself, nor have asked riches for yourself, nor have asked the life of your enemies, but have asked for yourself understanding to discern justice, **¹²** behold, I have done according to your words; see, I have given you a wise and understanding heart, so that there has not been anyone like you before you, nor shall any like you arise after you."

5. **Faithfulness**: Faithful leaders trust in God's plans and are steadfast in their commitment. Abraham's faith is a prime example (Hebrews 11:8-12). "**⁸** By faith Abraham obeyed when he was called to go out to the place which he would receive as an inheritance. And he went out, not knowing where he was going. **⁹** By faith he dwelt in the land of promise as *in* a foreign country, dwelling in tents with Isaac and Jacob, the heirs with him of the same promise; **¹⁰** for he waited for the city which has foundations, whose builder and maker *is* God.

[11] By faith Sarah herself also received strength to conceive seed, and she[a] bore a child when she was past the age, because she judged Him faithful who had promised. [12] Therefore, from one man, and him as good as dead, were born *as many* as the stars of the sky in multitude—innumerable as the sand which is by the seashore."

6. **Courage:** Biblical leaders are often called to lead with courage, even in the face of adversity. Joshua was instructed to be strong and courageous (Joshua 1:9). "[9] Have I not commanded you? Be strong and of good courage; do not be afraid, nor be dismayed, for the Lord your God *is* with you wherever you go."

7. **Compassion:** Compassionate leaders care deeply for their people, as seen in Jesus' empathy for the sick and needy (Matthew 9:36). "[36] But when He saw the multitudes, He was moved with compassion for them, because they were [a]weary and scattered, like sheep having no shepherd."

8. **Patience:** Patience is a critical trait, especially during trials and waiting on God's timing. David displayed patience while waiting to become king (Psalm 40:1-2). "I waited patiently for the Lord; and He inclined to me, and heard my cry. [2] He also brought me up out of a horrible pit, out of the miry clay, and set my feet upon a rock, and established my steps."

9. **Vision:** Having a clear, God-inspired vision helps leaders guide their people effectively. Nehemiah had a vision to rebuild Jerusalem's walls (Nehemiah 2:17). "[17] Then I said to them, "You see the distress that we *are* in, how Jerusalem

lies [a]waste, and its gates are burned with fire. Come and let us build the wall of Jerusalem, that we may no longer be a reproach."

10. **Dependence on God**: A strong reliance on God for guidance and strength is fundamental. Leaders like Daniel depended on prayer and God's wisdom (Daniel 6:10)."[10] Now when Daniel knew that the writing was signed, he went home. And in his upper room, with his windows open toward Jerusalem, he knelt down on his knees three times that day, and prayed and gave thanks before his God, as was his custom since early days."

These qualities not only guide effective leadership but also reflect a deep, spiritual connection with God, inspiring others to follow with faith and commitment. If there's a particular quality you'd like to explore further or relate to a specific biblical leader, let me know!

7.1 Joshua—an Old Testament Model

Although the Scriptures contain numerous excellent leadership models, most organizations have not always appreciated or followed them. Without a deep understanding and appreciation of these models, it is highly likely that you will conform to a misguided approach that will often prove ineffective and unsuccessful.

When it comes to Old Testament models of leadership, I cannot think of any person more appropriate to illustrate this point than Joshua. Joshua provides an excellent example of the Old Testament model of a leader. He encapsulated all the relevant concepts of leadership, both as a follower and a leader. Here is a history of the man and his journey from a willing assistant and dedicated servant to a successful commander and chief.

Joshua was the son of Nun. His original name was Hoshea, which means salvation **(See Numbers 13:8),** but Moses changed his name to Yehoshua, which is translated *Yahweh is salvation.* **(See Numbers 3:16.)** He is also called Yeshua, a shortened form of Yehoshua. The name Joshua is the Hebrew counterpart to the Greek name Lesous, commonly known as Jesus, which establishes Joshua as a prefiguring figure of Christ. To gain deeper insights into what contributed to Joshua's effectiveness as Israel's leader, let's explore several pivotal moments from his life and leadership journey. Through these scenes, we can uncover the qualities and experiences that shaped him into a formidable guide for his people.

7.2 Joshua Emerged as a Leader

The first point I want to draw to your attention is that Joshua emerged as a leader. He did not just arrive on the scene one day, announcing himself as a top-ranking army general desiring a high position. We have never seen or heard of him behaving as though he were more capable than his predecessor and mentor. According to the scriptures, Joshua was chosen by Moses, and, probably more importantly, this came as a result of Moses' request to God to provide a successor to lead the people after his departure. **(See Numbers 27:16-17).**

It is also notable that God directed him to Joshua, whom he had already mentored for several years. Therefore, every leader must identify prospective candidates as they emerge from obscurity and, as directed by God, reach a place of prominence.

For at least forty years before Moses' death, God trained Joshua under Moses' guidance to lead the people into the Promised Land. So you can see here that one of the primary qualifications for successful leadership becomes evident through a selection and mentoring process.

Joshua is first mentioned in **Exodus 17:8–16,** where Moses selects him to lead the Israelite army into battle against the Amalekites. Again, it is worth noting that early on, Moses recognized Joshua's leadership qualities. At the same time, God was equipping Joshua to be a warrior, as both leadership and warfare skills were essential to successfully leading the people into the Promised Land.

He is next mentioned in **Exodus 24:13,** where he accompanied Moses up the mountain to receive the Ten Commandments. From then on, Joshua became Moses' assistant, and Moses became his mentor. I am saying here that a mentor-protégé relationship is essential to the emerging process of becoming an effective spiritual leader. Joshua easily fulfills his role as a protégé.

The next step in his emerging process is that Joshua stood guard at the tent of meeting, where Moses met face to face with God (**Exodus 33:11**). Accordingly, he would have observed how God dealt with Moses and vice versa. That kind of exposure would certainly encourage his grasp of the leadership exhibition he was destined to undertake. Can you see how important it is to emerge with adequate leadership training and development? It is much more beneficial than appearing on the scene one day unannounced to take over. In essence, training and development are essential under the watchful eyes of someone with a reputable character if you are going to succeed as a leader in your role.

Also, Joshua was one of the twelve spies Moses chose to spy out the land of Canaan. **(See Numbers 13:8.)** He was one of the only two (he and Caleb), who returned with a good report. The Bible says they both tore their clothing at the bad report from the other ten and urged the Israelites not to rebel against the Lord. (See **Numbers 14:6–9.)** Consequently, because of their faith in God, only Caleb and Joshua, the original 2.5 million people who departed Egypt, were allowed to enter the Promised Land. (See **Numbers 14:38.)** As you can see, rebellion and disobedience are not a great idea if you are to be a good representation of a leader. Under no circumstances should you rebel against God or those whom God set over you. Pride leads followers to believe they are more capable than those God has chosen and placed in leadership positions.

7.3 Character and Authority Test

The next aspect of his life that made Joshua an ultimate model and can also be considered part of the emerging process is evident in his character test. Joshua's character had to be tested and proven in various leadership situations. For instance, he developed a personal and independent relationship with God. He received revelations from Him before the Lord was ready to ordain and raise him up to a more prominent leadership position. All this took place *before* Moses' death. (See **Numbers 27:18–23.)** In addition, at God's command, Moses had Joshua stand before the priest Eleazar, who commissioned him before all the people. Moses laid hands on him and imparted his authority to him. From then on, no one could question the authenticity of Joshua's appointment as a leader of the children of Israel.

But if you want to know how Joshua's character was tested and proven, notice what happened after Moses' death. Joshua would not move into position until God visited and reaffirmed him as the leader. Most of us would not have waited to hear what God had to say—but Joshua understood the magnitude of the task and the importance of taking instructions from God. **Joshua 1:1–18 tells us:**

> *"After the death of Moses, the servant of the Lord, it came to pass that the Lord spoke to Joshua, the son of Nun, Moses' assistant, saying: "Moses My servant is dead. Now therefore, arise, go over this Jordan, you and all this people, to the land which I am giving to them—the children of Israel. Every place that the sole of your foot will tread upon, I have given you, as I said to Moses. ⁴ From the wilderness and this Lebanon as far as the great river, the River Euphrates, all the land of the Hittites, and to the Great Sea toward the going down of the sun shall be your territory. No man shall be able to stand before you all the days of your life; as I was with Moses, so I will be with you. I will not leave you nor forsake you. Be strong and of a good courage, for to this people you will divide as an inheritance the land which I swore to their fathers to give them. Only be strong and very courageous, that you may observe to do according to all the law which Moses my servant commanded you; do not turn from it to the right hand or to the left that you may prosper wherever you go. This Book of the Law shall not depart from your mouth, but you shall meditate in it day and night, that*

you may observe to do according to all that is written in it. For then you will make your way prosperous, and then you will have good success. Have I not commanded you? Be strong and of good courage; do not be afraid, nor be dismayed, for the Lord your God is with you wherever you go."

This passage highlights a vital truth—that an outstanding leader waits for instruction from the Lord before making any move. For reasons such as this, spiritual leaders must be called and trained by God. By the time Joshua assumed leadership, he was eighty years old and had been Moses' assistant for forty years. As we can see, an effective leader is always the result of sound preparation and encouragement, just as Joshua was the result of Moses' ongoing mentorship. It is crucial to note that he did not start acting like a leader only because he was assigned a position; he developed over time.

This is one of the greatest challenges facing leaders today. Many have been in their positions for years but have not been properly trained, nor are they training others to replace them when they are gone. Moses is our model here; he groomed Joshua for forty years. John Maxwell said, "The success of a leader can only be measured by his successors." And if you have done your job well, your successor should be able to do an even more excellent job than you when you are gone. This is evident in Moses' case; he led the children of Israel out of slavery and trained Joshua, who led them into the Promised Land. In essence, he took them out but needed a Joshua to take them in. This is a pattern we see in scripture time and again. For example, Elijah mentored Elisha, who performed twice as many miracles as his predecessor. David served under King Saul but eventually became the greatest king of Israel.

"Saul has slain his thousands And David his ten thousand" **1 Samuel 18:7**. It was this very principle Jesus shared in **John 14:12** when He declared, "Most assuredly, I say to you, he who believes in Me, the works that I do he will do also; and greater *works* than these he will do, because I go to My Father."

In his book *The 21 Irrefutable Laws of Leadership,* John Maxwell refers to this as the law of legacy: "When all is said and done, your ability as a leader will be judged by how well your people and your organization did after you were gone. Your lasting value will be measured by succession." He said, "To create a legacy, you need to be strategic and intentional." Then, he suggested some guidelines. For example, decide ahead of time what you are willing to give up, take the initiative to start the process, know your goals with each person, and finally prepare to pass on the baton."

Clearly, it is essential for leaders to train others to replace them when they are absent. "The worst tragedy imaginable occurs when someone makes a great impact for the kingdom only to leave no one to carry on his legacy when they are gone." A leader who leaves his people without a successor is only insecure and self-centered.

7.4 Joshua was Committed

Joshua not only emerged as a leader or was tested in character, but, as with Moses and David, he was also committed. Therefore, not only do you need to be chosen, anointed, and appointed, but you must possess this vital personal character trait; you must be committed. In **Numbers 14:28** we see that Joshua had a history of faithful commitment and was described as a man of spiritual perception and faith. Let's look at some of the other qualities that made him a great candidate for leadership.

7.5 Joshua was Submissive

When I consider the difference between the attributes and style of Joshua and Moses, I am astounded by the excellent servant's attitude Joshua must have maintained. He remained submissive to the order of rank, so to speak, and never once attempted to displace Moses' leadership. Even after Moses was old and could no longer do what he could have done, Joshua simply waited until it was his turn to take authority. Based on observation and experience, you would have to search the world over to discover characters such as Joshua's. Most would not hesitate to organize a faction to get rid of Moses with little or no hesitation. The point is, would we do as Joshua did in our day? I doubt it very much.

The fact is, in this Twenty-First Century society, Moses would have been replaced by someone younger, physically stronger, and, from a human perspective, seen as more capable, whether he was God's choice or not. I can assure you that this is not God's plan, so please do not ever consider it.

7.6 Joshua was Courageous

According to Joshua Chapter One, God commanded Joshua to "be strong and courageous" at least four times in this chapter. Not only that, but God also told Joshua twice before Moses died to "be strong and courageous" (**Deuteronomy 31:6-7**). And again, when the Lord authorized him, He told Joshua to "be strong and courageous"

(**Deuteronomy 31:23**). Even the elders of Israel joined in charging Joshua to "be strong and courageous" (**Joshua 1:18**).

Why do you think God repeatedly told Joshua to be strong and courageous? Here are some likely reasons; the list is not exhaustive.

Firstly, God knew Joshua would need strength and courage to face challenges like never before if he was going to succeed in taking the Promised Land. You, too, will need to be courageous if you are going to succeed in bringing God's people into their destiny and purpose.

Secondly, God told Joshua to be strong and courageous because he would have to take the land, and capturing it would not be easy. (**Joshua 1:6**). He would need courage and lots of it. Numerous hurdles were to be expected. The first was the Jordan, a dangerous impasse during the spring. And if that were not bad enough, once the Jordan crossed, Joshua would face Jericho, a walled city, and to make matters worse, he had no machinery or skilled labor force to take the walls down. In addition, the land was inhabited, which meant resistance (war) was to be expected. And worse still, he had a whole bunch of obstinate and unwilling people to deal with. Contrary to what you may think, leading people will never be like a bed of roses.

Third, God told Joshua to be strong and courageous because he would need to obey God's law: "only be strong and very courageous, that you may observe to do according to all the law which Moses My servant commanded you; do not turn from it to the right hand or the left, that you may prosper wherever you go." (**Joshua 1:7**). Prosperity and leadership success are a direct result of obeying the word of God. In other words, you will find success and prosperity through the wisdom and knowledge of the word of God.

Finally, God told Joshua to be strong and courageous because he would not have to do it alone. He had divine assistance. The Lord Himself would be with him. "Have I not commanded you? Be strong and of good courage; do not be afraid, nor be dismayed, for the Lord your God is with you wherever you go." (**Joshua 1:9**).

Effective leadership demands immense perseverance and courage, especially when the journey feels arduous and enjoyment seems distant. In such challenging times, it's incredibly comforting to recognize that divine assistance is at play, offering guidance and support. This unshakeable presence can embolden a leader to continue pressing forward, providing the strength needed to navigate through difficulties with unwavering resolve.

As Joshua was called to conquer a land, so are you called to conquer the world. Our calling is to make disciples of every nation, except that we are not fighting a physical war. We do not fight against flesh and blood (**Eph. 6:12**), for the weapons of our warfare are not carnal—but mighty through God for the pulling down of strongholds. (**2 Cor. 10:4**). Despite this, the need for strength and courage remains very essential.

Joshua was, in essence, a military leader with a leadership style far different from Moses'. However, Joshua must have decided not to imitate Moses' style but to be himself. He took command when Israel needed a military commander, not diplomatic authority.

How, then, did Joshua become courageous? Joshua became courageous in the following ways and is an *example* for us today.

He obtained courage partly through his fellowship and association with Moses. He attached himself to Moses, the meek servant of the Lord. He saw Moses work, heard him speak, observed him seeking the face of God, and watched him pray and in prayer.

Joshua also obtained courage through intimacy *with God*. He followed his mentor and spent valuable time in the Lord's presence. All this I highlight to say that we, too, are to follow the same pattern. **Exodus 33:7-11** explains;

> *"Moses took his tent and pitched it outside the camp, far from the camp, and called it the tabernacle of meeting. And it came to pass that everyone who sought the Lord went out to the tabernacle of meeting which was outside the camp. So it was, whenever Moses went out to the tabernacle, that all the people rose, and each man stood at his tent door and watched Moses until he had gone into the tabernacle. And it came to pass, when Moses entered the tabernacle that the pillar of cloud descended and stood at the door of the tabernacle, and the Lord talked with Moses. All the people saw the pillar of cloud standing at the tabernacle door, and all the people rose and worshiped, each man in his tent door. So the Lord spoke to Moses face to face, as a man speaks to his friend. And he would return to the camp, but his servant Joshua the son of Nun, a young man, did not depart from the tabernacle."*

Notice that after Moses returned from the camp, "the young man Joshua, the son of Nun, did not leave the tent." This is significant because it implies that Joshua had a deep hunger and a great appetite for the Lord's presence. It is almost as though he had made the tabernacle a dwelling place, and; "He that dwells in the secret place of the Most High shall abide under the shadow of the Almighty." (**Psalm 91:1**) Joshua learned to live in the presence of the Lord, where he found strength and courage! It is no wonder he became courageous and strong. We, too, are to spend more valuable time in His presence and to develop a passion and hunger for more of Him. As Jesus said in **Matthew 5:6**, "Blessed are those who hunger and thirst for righteousness, for they shall be filled." Filled with His love for his people, His power to lead His people, and His grace to endure the challenges to be encountered. In essence, the way to success is to live in close fellowship with God.

Moreover, Joshua did all this with faith and confidence in God's promise. God gave him His *Word* that he would be with him, go before him, and drive out his enemies before him. He believed in God and felt satisfied and confident in the victory promised by God. Following the death of Moses, the pillar of the cloud was withdrawn as it was no longer necessary, but to God be the glory, the Ark of the Covenant and the mercy seat remained. The presence of God was still in the camp, and as long as God's presence is with you, success is inevitable.

Faith will make any man courageous, bold, and strong. Nothing can intimidate, discourage, or reverse the confidence of a committed leader standing on the promises of God! Therefore, when you know that the Lord is present in all of your endeavors, you can go ahead in confidence and conquer the opposition and the world. In reality, your enemy is defeated, and you can consider your life a success. Glory be to God.

It was not only by faith that Joshua became courageous, but according to James Smith 1826, "it was also by the power of prayer. Like all devoted people, he had 'power with God.' He first fought his battles on his knees before the mercy seat; he <u>conquered</u> his foes in secret, before God, and then met them in the open field and chased them as the lion hunts its prey. If you can succeed with *God*, you will surely prevail with *men*. What begins with powerful prayer is sure to end with joyful praise". In addition to his fellowship with Moses, his intimacy with God, his faith in the promise, and his power in prayer, Joshua was favored with the assistance of the great Captain of Salvation. Hence, we read,

> *"And it came to pass, when Joshua was by Jericho, that he lifted his eyes and looked, and behold, a Man stood opposite him with His sword drawn in His hand. And Joshua went to Him and said to Him, "Are You for our adversaries or for us?" So He said, "No, but as Commander of the army of the Lord I have now come." And Joshua fell on his face to the earth and worshiped, and said to Him, "What does my Lord say to His servant?"* **(Joshua 5:13-14)**

This was one of the many occasions Jesus showed up in Old Testament times; He was there to assure Joshua that He was with him. He showed up to encourage the people and to teach Joshua "to whom the glory of his victories would be due." When intimacy with God has become a habit, and when we hold on to faith in God's promise. When we make prayer our number one priority, then Jesus will show up to empower us. He has given His words of assurance, such as, "Surely, I am with you always! I will never leave you nor forsake you! My strength is made perfect in your weakness!" There is, therefore, no need to fear, for the

Lord our God is with us.

In a demonstration of his courage and reliance on God, Joshua obeyed the Lord at Jericho. First, he circumcised the people, and second, he marched around the city for seven days carrying the Ark of the Covenant in total obedience to God. The result was that the walls of Jericho collapsed, and the first city of the Promised Land was captured—Hallelujah! And that was to be their first taste of victory.

It did not matter to Joshua what the inhabitants of Jericho might say or think concerning his unusual operation outside the city walls. He was moving in obedience to God's command, and nothing else mattered. This is our example; we are to follow God's command despite others' opinions.

Joshua was victorious in conquering the land according to God's promise. He led Israel into the Promised Land and divided it among them. "His courage never failed him. His *God* never forsook him. His *enemies* never prevailed against him, except where a disobedient follower committed a trespass, such as in the case of Achan, **Joshua 7**. In his final address to the nation, he called his people to witness by telling them, "Behold, this day I *am* going the way of all the earth. And you know in all your hearts and souls that not one thing has failed of all the good things the Lord your God spoke about you. All have come to pass for you; not one word of them has failed." This is one of the reasons you cannot afford to fail, and neither can you conceive the thought that you can fail. Everything that God has promised you shall come to pass.

7.7 Joshua was willing to pay the Price

As a leader, Joshua did "whatever it took" to succeed. He practiced the law of submission, and his no-nonsense leadership style drove him to pay whatever price was necessary to get the job done. He was willing to take any essential risks without hesitation. He asked the doubters, "How long will you neglect to go and possess the land which the Lord God of your fathers has given you?" **(Joshua 18:3).** He could not understand why they hesitated; why didn't they just go and possess the land God had promised them? Does that sound like you? Are you someone who procrastinates when it comes to possessing your inheritance? Why don't you arise and take possession of God's will for your life? Don't you know you are not what the devil says you are? You are not what the world says you are; you are what the living word says you are. You are more than a conqueror through Christ, who loves you. You are the head and not the tail; you are above and not beneath, glory to God.

7.8 Joshua Listened and Obeyed

Joshua was not only willing to pay the price but was also obedient. When God spoke, Joshua not only listened but obeyed. His attitude became an example for the people and should be the same for us today. As stated earlier, his obedience to God was evident after crossing the Jordon on dry ground. God commanded the people to conquer the city by marching around it thirteen times in silence before blowing their trumpets and shouting. As leaders, sometimes we need to quit speaking and listen to and follow the Lord's commands. Joshua and his people gained victory by following God's unique battle strategy.

(See Joshua 6.) We also know that in a later battle against the Amorites, Joshua demonstrated even greater faith in God when he commanded the sun to stand still to help them win the war (see Joshua 10.)

Chapter Summary

Joshua was an outstanding model of leadership, embodying the essence of leading with integrity and vision. His approach was characterized by a remarkable blend of strength and compassion, as he navigated challenges with unwavering determination while always considering the needs of those he led. Each decision he made reflected a deep understanding of his team's strengths and weaknesses, showcasing a commitment to growth and collaboration. His ability to inspire and motivate others not only fostered loyalty but also cultivated a sense of shared purpose, making him a model leader. Please note the following scenes from his life:

- He did not just arrive on the scene nor force Moses out of his place to gain a leadership position.

- He emerged as a leader and conducted himself with wisdom and humility.

- He succeeded when his character was tested.

- He was committed.

- He was submissive.

- He was courageous.

- He was willing to pay the price, and probably more importantly;

- He was an obedient and dedicated visionary, a servant of God.

Check List

Having established himself as a man of faith and courage, Joshua and Caleb brought back a positive report recorded in Numbers 13 after spying on the land.

1. He was a brilliant military leader and a strong spiritual influence, but his submission to God was key to his success.

2. Reviewing the leadership qualities demonstrated by Joshua's life, we can see that he was a man of great spiritual perception and faith. In the same way, every spiritual leader must lean on God and acknowledge Him in every way, rather than merely relying on their fallible human understanding and abilities. (See **Proverbs 3:5-6.**)

3. Finally, Joshua listened to God and obeyed His commands. He was confident in God's strength, courageous in the face of opposition, and willing to seek God's advice.

4. Under Joshua's capable leadership, the people learned that victory came through faith in God and obedience to His Word rather than military might or numerical superiority. Some trust in chariots and horses, but we will remember the name

of the Lord our God. **Psalm 20:7.**

To be strong and courageous leaders like Joshua, we must also be ready to listen and respond to God's instructions. Once we have His instruction, we must diligently carry it out to move in the power of His Spirit.

Exercise

Evaluate your leadership style and answer the following questions:

1. What can I learn from Joshua's leadership qualities?

2. Do you consider yourself to be a person of vision and faith? state your reasons

3. Explain how you emerged as a leader.

4. Do you have, or have you ever had, a personal mentor? Explain.

5. Describe and evaluate the model set by Joshua.

Personal Notes

_____

_____

_____

_____

Chapter Eight
NEW TESTAMENT MODEL OF LEADERSHIP

Jesus—A New Testament Model

Among the figures presented in the New Testament, none exemplifies the qualities of effective leadership better than Jesus Christ Himself.

For individuals who may not possess a comprehensive understanding of His identity, allow me to provide a succinct overview. Christians who hold the Bible as sacred scripture universally recognize Jesus as the eternal and uniquely begotten Son of the living God. He is revered not only as the just and sovereign ruler of both heaven and earth but also as a multifaceted presence in the lives of believers. Jesus is acknowledged as our Lord, the guiding Master who leads us, the Redeemer who offers salvation, the Savior who rescues us from despair, and the Friend who provides unwavering support and companionship.

The New Testament describes Him as the Jews' long-awaited Messiah and the living fulfillment of Old Testament prophecies. This is to say, Jesus did not just arrive on the scene at the time of His birth about two thousand years ago, as some would have us believe. He is from the beginning; **John 1:1-5** explains it like this;

"In the beginning was the Word, and the Word was with God, and the Word was God. He was in the beginning with God. All things were made through Him, and without Him nothing was made that was made. In Him was life, and the life was the light of men. And the light shines in the darkness, and the darkness did not comprehend it."

The Apostle Paul in **Colossians 1:18** declares Him as "the head of the body, the church, who is the beginning, the firstborn from the dead, that in all things He may have the pre-eminence." This makes Him the ultimate model for spiritual leadership, which is why we are to pay special attention to the examples He left us. Here are a few critical observations from His earthly journey.

8.1 Preparation

One of the first and most significant observations about Christ's leadership occurred at the beginning of his ministry. John Maxwell referred to this in his book ***The 21 Irrefutable Laws of Leadership*** as the law of sacrifice. In **Matthew 4:1-11** we see Jesus being prepared for leadership and the place where it all began, "the wilderness." The Bible specifically pointed out that it was the Holy Spirit that led Jesus out into the wilderness right after His baptism to be tempted by the devil. This reminds us that at least part of our preparation and processing for ministry occurs through a wilderness experience. In other words, you should be able to identify a wilderness experience as part of your leadership journey.

By the way, this is what leading is all about. It's about leading the way through the rugged terrain of life's journey—either because you know the way, have been there before, or know how to get there. And as mentioned before, leaders who do not know the way are blind leaders of the blind.

The most obvious question to ask here is, if I can't identify with a wilderness experience, should I go ahead and manufacture one? The answer is no. Notice that the Bible says that the Holy Spirit led Jesus into the wilderness. I believe every leader called by God would have been led by the Spirit to experience a wilderness. The difference is that you may not have identified it for what it was. But just in case this has not been your experience, don't worry; if you hang around long enough, you too will inevitably have to face your no man's land or your period of disfavor.

The devil tempted Jesus for forty days in the wilderness. This test demonstrated whether Jesus would quit or stand on the word.

Considering that Jesus was God in the flesh, you may want to ask whether it was necessary for Him to go through such an experience. The answer is probably not; he didn't need it. But He did it as an example for us. On the other hand, however, if Jesus needed to go through the wilderness, why shouldn't you and I? And just in case you are wondering, here is the reason. In his book "The Name of Jesus," Henry Nouwen highlights that Jesus' three temptations reflect the challenges leaders encounter today.

1. **To be Self-Sufficient**

The first temptation was to be self-sufficient, as demonstrated by the saying, 'Command these stones be made bread.' But Jesus resisted any notion of self-sufficiency. He often explained that He never did anything without consulting His Father. We, too, must resist this temptation. Every leader must rely on God to supply all our needs according to his riches in glory through Christ Jesus.

1. **To be Spectacular**

The second temptation here was to be spectacular (**Matthew 4:5-7**): "**Then the devil took Him up into the holy city, set Him on the pinnacle of the temple, and said to Him,** 'If You are the Son of God, throw Yourself down. For it is written: 'He shall give His angels charge over you,' and, 'in *their* hands, they shall bear you up, lest you dash your foot against a stone.'" Jesus said to him, "It is written again, 'You shall not tempt the Lord your God.'"

The devil asked Jesus to show off His skills, but because He was secure in His identity as the Son of God, Jesus once again refused. You, too, must be secure in your identity as a son of God. You do not need to put your gifts, talents, or skills on display to please the devil or anyone else. Remember, you can do all things but only through Christ; otherwise, you are acting in your own selfish pride.

1. **The Chance to Gain Power**

Finally, the tempter would offer Jesus the chance to obtain power. In **Matthew 4:8-11,** we see: "Again, the devil took Him up on an exceedingly high mountain, and showed Him all the kingdoms of the world and their glory. And he said to Him, 'All these things I will give You if You will fall down and worship me.' Then Jesus said to him, "Away with you, Satan! For it is written, 'you shall worship the Lord your God, and Him only you shall serve." Then the devil left Him, and behold, angels came and ministered to Him.' Notice that Jesus didn't take the shortcut to gain power or worship." He resisted the temptation, and so should you.

Can you see why you cannot afford to grab every opportunity you get to gain power? For example, taking it by force or claiming self-appointed leadership could be a shortcut that ultimately plays right into the enemy's hands.

Every leader must live at a higher level than others, which is why they must go through a very important preparation phase before they can reap the great rewards of success. It is during this preparation season that you are tested to discover whether you can live at that higher level. No one responded better to that challenge than Jesus. He did not fall for the temptation to be self-sufficient, He did not fall for the temptation to show off His skills, and neither did He fall for the temptation to gain power. It is reasonable to say He passed His tests with maximum success during the preparation stage.

8.2 Choosing and Developing Team Members

Immediately following the commencement of His public ministry, Jesus (see **Matt. 4:12-25**) demonstrated one of the most outstanding examples of His leadership when He called twelve other leaders to join Him. He called them disciples and immediately began training them to become future leaders of the Church. The objective was to reproduce His leadership skills in others. Notice the first people He chose; he chose three fishermen and gave them a vision for spiritual reproduction: He said, "Follow me, and I will make you fishers of men." **(Matt. 4:19).** Clearly, He was calling these men to be leaders, as well. Remember, you cannot neglect choosing and developing other leaders. It does not matter their background and/or their social status; with proper training and development, they will be transformed into honorable vessels God can use for His glory.

So what can we learn about the way Jesus selected and developed leaders? Well, it's clear that they were not necessarily people with the principal human credentials for leaders, as pointed out earlier. They were ordinary, everyday people. Jesus was walking by the Sea of Galilee when He saw them plying their trade nearby. **(See Matt 4:18.)** He identified them as potential leaders and called them to follow Him and to become leaders themselves. Speaking to them in a language they understood, He said, "I will make you fishers of men." He was challenging them to join Him in catching men rather than fish.

Effective leaders always attract and factor in others' talents. In other words, leaders must train and equip others to reach their full potential, and no one did it better than Jesus. In **Matt. 9:37-38,** we see Jesus' vision for even more workers, "the harvest truly is plentiful, but laborers are few. Therefore, pray the Lord of the harvest to send out laborers into His harvest." Then, in **Matthew Chapter 10,** even though Jesus had not finished training His disciples, He sent them out to exercise their gifts, and we should learn from His example. At some point, you need to cease lecturing and send people out to try what they have learned. Now, let's look at how Jesus empowered His twelve disciples.

Notice in **Matthew 10:1-4** that Jesus gave his disciples a personal invitation, and the next move was to empower them. Then He gave them a direct order; that is, after instructing them, He sent them out with clear instructions. **Matthew 10:7:** "As you go, preach saying, the kingdom of heaven is at hand. Heal the sick, cleanse the leper, raise the dead, cast out demons, freely you have received, freely give."

This is the ultimate example of excellent communication and the true essence of a successful leader. The true leader does it not only for a reward but also because they are called and have a passion for it.

8.3 Jesus Taught Servant Leadership

As mentioned earlier, the fundamental essence of spiritual leadership is servanthood; Jesus himself is our ultimate example. He undertook the task of changing the lives of those who would come thousands of years after Him, and He succeeded. "He did it without writing any books, building any schools, or establishing any institutions." So if Jesus chose to deposit His legacy in people, we should learn and practice His method. He did this through instruction, demonstration, experience, and assessment.

Those who are in authority Lord it over them, but it shall not be so among you.

Jesus ably demonstrated this truth about servanthood in **Matthew 20:25-28.** The mother of Zebedee's sons brought them to Jesus with a request. She asked Jesus to allow one of her sons to sit at His right hand and the other at His left in His kingdom, taking positions of power and authority.

The disciples did not realize that a life of service marks God's kingdom and rejects every form of personal ambition, power, prominence, and domination. In verses 25-27, Jesus describes the hierarchical and oppressive power

> "Those who are in authority Lord it over them, but it shall not be so among you."

of the elite in the secular world. "Its domination is accomplished by intimidation, military power, taxation, and a small group of decision-makers that control society for its benefit." **(See the New Interpreters Study Bible.)** Look at Jesus' response to their request in v. 25-27: "Those who are in authority lord it over them, but it shall not be so among you."

The fundamental lesson taught here is found in **Matthew 20:28:** "Just as the son of man did not come to be served, but to serve, and to give his life as a ransom for many." Jesus is indeed our ultimate model of leadership. He did not lead by barking out orders or by enforcing His authority over others. He led by serving alongside His followers. "He that will be great in the kingdom of God, let him be your servant" **(Matthew 20:26)**. And remember, when you are looking to fill a leadership position, look for those who are willing to serve, not for those who are impressed with themselves, their degrees, eloquence or financial advantage. Let it be the one willing to sweep the floor and pick up the trash. That's how Jesus describes the greatest among us.

In Jesus' day, the roads were mostly unpaved and therefore dusty, so their feet always needed washing. The job of washing feet was assigned to the lowest of servants. Despite this tradition, at the Last Supper, Jesus humbled himself by washing the disciples' feet.

"And supper being ended, the devil having already put it into the heart of Judas Iscariot, Simon's son, to betray Him, Jesus, knowing that the Father had given all things into His hands and that He had come from God and was going to God, rose from supper and laid aside His garments, took a towel and girded Himself. After that, He poured water into a basin and began to wash the disciples' feet, and to wipe them with the towel with which He was girded. Then He came to Simon Peter. And Peter said to Him, "Lord, are You washing my feet?" Jesus answered and said to him, what I am doing you do not understand now, but you will know after this." After this, he said to them, "Do you understand what I have done for you? You call me Lord and Master, and rightly so, for that is what I am. Now that I, your Lord and Master, have washed your feet, you also should wash one another's feet. I have set you an example that you should follow as I have done for you. I tell you the truth; no servant is greater than his master, nor is a messenger greater than the one who sent him. Now that you know these things, you will be blessed if you do them" **(John 13:12-17)**.

In essence, successful spiritual leadership requires humility and a heartfelt commitment to embracing tasks others might shy away from. This dedication not only strengthens our communities but also fosters a deep sense of connection and support among us all.

A Need for Privacy and Replenishment

Finally, it is very important that leaders schedule valuable time for reclusiveness and replenishment. This means you should not always allow others to dictate your agenda. You should not be prevented from taking time out to pray and seek the face of God to recharge. Jesus demonstrated this lesson with excellence. Despite what others might have thought, He would often leave the demands of His work to go away and pray. As the following sequence of events illustrates, he used the privacy in God's presence to gain insight. In **Mark 1:24-34,** it was the end of the day, but the crowd was preparing to increase their demands, which meant He was being pressured to meet their every need. In the morning, however, in **Mark 1:35,** He left the middle of His ministry to go and pray, leaving some unmet needs. As ironic as it may appear to be, Jesus needed to retreat and get away from the crowd to regain His store of energy and anointing before He could continue to minister. It is abundantly clear in **verse 38** that "once He declared His purpose, His Father renewed His perspective and gave Him new direction." This means His priority was His Father's business rather than anything else. You might say that maintaining His priorities gave Him the strength and power to be effective in His ministerial capacity. How much more do we mere mortals need to get our priorities right?

Evaluate your situation:

Critically evaluate your leadership style and compare **it** with those mentioned above. Ask yourself the following questions as a guideline:

- Do you think you offer any of the required attributes?

- Have you had any wilderness training?

- What is your attitude when faced with complex challenges? Do you readily accept challenges as part of the training process to build your character?

- Do you lead by example?

- Do you consider yourself above the tasks you ask others to do?

- What are the benefits of leading by example? Does it encourage cooperation?

- Do you get people to be responsible and to take responsibility?

Exercise

1. What can you learn from Jesus' leadership qualities?

2. Do you consider yourself to be a person of vision and faith?

3. Describe and evaluate the model set by Jesus.

Personal Notes

_____
_____
_____
_____
_____

SECTION FOUR

HOW TO INCREASE YOUR PROSPECT OF SUCCESS WITH IMMEDIATE EFFECT

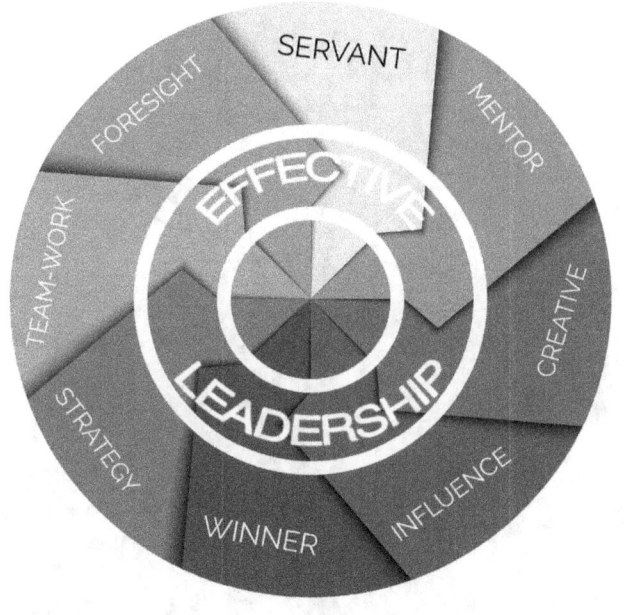

CHAPTERS 9 – 11

HOW TO GAIN TRUE LEADERSHIP

WITH INSTANTANEOUS RESULTS

Chapter Nine
HOW TO INCREASE YOUR PROSPECT OF SUCCESS WITH IMMEDIATE EFFECT

President Barack Obama once said, "Success will not come if you wait for some other person or some other time." And Dale Carnegie said, "Discouragement and failure are two of the surest stepping stones to success." The fact is—you have the power to increase your prospect of success with immediate effects. What you cannot afford is to sit around waiting for other people or for some other time. And neither should you allow discouragement and failure to stand in your way. Applying the following golden rules and spiritual principles will help you build a solid foundation and set you up to achieve outstanding accomplishments.

9.1 Principle Number 1—Lead and not manage

If you want to increase your chances of success with immediate effects, one of the first and most important principles you must grasp is the difference between the leader and the manager. Not only do you need to know the difference, but it is crucial that you understand that spiritually dynamic leaders lead, not manage, although they are complementary.

According to "The Wall Street Journal Guide to Management" by Alan Murray, published by Harper Business. "Leadership and management are not the same thing but must go hand in hand and are complementary."

The manager's role is to plan, organize and coordinate. The leader's role is to inspire and motivate. In his 1989 book "On Becoming a Leader," Warren Bennis proposed a list of the differences:

- The manager administers; the leader innovates.

- The manager is a copy; the leader is an original.

- The manager maintains; the leader develops.

- The manager focuses on systems and structure; the leader focuses on people.

- The manager relies on control; the leader inspires trust.

- The manager has a short-range view; the leader has a long-range perspective.

- The manager asks how and when; the leader asks what and why.

- The manager always has his or her eye on the bottom line; the leader's eye is on the horizon.

- The manager imitates; the leader originates.

- The manager accepts the status quo; the leader challenges it.

- The manager is the classic good soldier; the leader is his or her own person.

- The manager does things right; the leader does the right thing.

When most people think of leadership, they often picture an authoritarian in overall command, such as an aggressive military or boot camp commander with a raised voice demanding action. Others think of a manager closely supervising his staff, ensuring the work gets done. While these aspects may be part of leadership, they are not the essence of a true leader. As mentioned in chapter three, sub-section twelve, and in the references to the characters on how God raises leaders, the nature of spiritual leadership is exemplified by servant leadership, as illustrated and referenced above. When the mother of Zebedee's sons asked that her sons sit on either side of Jesus' throne in the kingdom of God, Jesus kindly but firmly told them that his leadership style stood in complete contrast to that of the world. Jesus taught that the greatest must be the servant; therefore, even if you do not understand much about leadership in general, under no circumstances should you miss this fundamental principle. In the words of John Maxwell, "As responsibilities increase, rights decrease."

Here is a Leadership Pyramid Based on this Principle as adapted from the John Maxwell Leadership Bible—Thomas Nelson Bibles 2286BG

"If the pyramid represents your life and the base represents the beginning of your leadership journey, your range of options is widest at the start. The younger you are, the more liberties you have with your time, vocabulary, money, etc. But as you grow into leadership, you deliberately surrender those rights and options. Keep in mind that servants push for no options and assume no rights as they work their way to the top."

9.2 Principle Number 2—Build Effective Relationships

As you have already discovered in this book, one of the primary functions of an effective leader is building successful relationships. After all, relationships will form the foundation of any successful organization. Remember—"If you are leading, and no one is following, you're only taking a walk." This is the reason people should be able to see God so clearly in you. Through your relationship with them, they want to give you their attention and help you achieve your goals, while inadvertently guiding them toward their own destinations. The question is, how do you build effective relationships?

A few years ago, my brother and I traveled in his vehicle in Kingston, Jamaica. A young man approached us at the traffic signal and asked if he could clean our car's windscreen in exchange for a small donation. My brother said no since our windscreen was already clean, but the young man insisted, "It's free for you today." Though I eventually gave him money, what I recall was my brother's comment. He said, "That's a good salesman." As a former insurance salesperson, he meant the young man knew his stuff—he was building a relationship so we wouldn't refuse his offer the next time we passed by. In other words, he was creating a network. The system he was creating was his business lifeline. For you, the network you are creating is your ministry or business support. Your network should include those above you, such as your bishop or mentor, etc., and those below you—your followers. It should also include family, friends, and unconnected people, such as those you meet casually wherever you go.

Contacts are potential prospective supporters waiting for you to connect with their needs. But the question is, how do you convert networks of contacts into supporters? You cannot afford to sit back, hoping they will remember meeting you previously at that networking event. Networking is a long-term investment. Do it right by adding value to the relationship, and that contact you just made can pay off—your success depends on it.

Relationships can be short-lived. No matter how charismatic you are, no one is likely to remember you from a business card or a one-time encounter. One of the biggest mistakes people make is that they often fail to follow up. It would be best if you established a connection from the beginning. Once you have met someone for the first time and established contact, send a "nice to meet you" text, e-mail, or any other social network means—such as Facebook, LinkedIn… etc. Remind your new contacts who you are, your area of expertise, your calling, and your passion for ministry or whatever it is you do. Human beings are too sociable to avoid building meaningful relationships—the only problem is you may not meet them at a mutually convenient time. For this reason, you have to find a way to keep you at the forefront of their mind. It is much easier for you to keep a connection alive than to bring it back to life once it has died. This means you have to take a pragmatic approach if you are going to turn your network of connections into interested participants. Social networking is the in thing nowadays—it keeps relationships strong, and it's free.

You can also build a relationship by establishing your reputation as an expert in your gifting or calling and by offering some free help and advice. Social networking is a cost-effective and easy way to stay on prospective supporters' minds, build their confidence in what you have to offer, and retain their support.

9.3 Principle Number 3—Lead with Discernment

It will undoubtedly spell disaster for the person who leads without the spirit of discernment. Discernment means to have awareness and understanding of your environment and the people around you. Discernment will enable you to make good and well-informed decisions, to decide between honesty and deceit, right and wrong. It is also the process of making careful distinctions in our thinking about sincerity. In other words, the ability to think with discernment is vital in the context of the decision-making process. And if you cannot discern, you are bound to make wrong conclusions. Here is how **1 John 4:1** explains it: "Beloved, do not believe every spirit, but test the spirits, whether they are of God; because many false prophets have gone out into the world. By this, you know the Spirit of God:" The Apostle John wants us to know that discernment is not optional for the believer in general and especially for the leader; it is an absolute necessity.

It means, therefore, that one of the keys to improving your prospect of success with immediate effects is the ability to exercise sound judgment, which will be based on operating in the spirit of discernment.

The fact is, if you fail to distinguish between truth and error, it is likely that you will make all manner of false judgments and compromises. This will subsequently lead to dissatisfaction among your followers. Unfortunately, discerning is an area where most leaders stumble. They exhibit little ability to distinguish fact from fiction, which is bound to lead to poor decision-making.

9.4 Principle Number 4—Lead with Passion

Former Secretary of State Henry Kissinger once said, "A leader does not deserve the name unless he is willing to stand alone." This means the leader must be so passionate about the work that he will stand alone if no one else stands with him. Passionate leaders are inspirational, motivating those they lead and the organization as a whole. The passionate leader, therefore, has an internal drive because he takes pleasure in his job. So, what are the advantages of a passionate leader?

- A passionate leader will always bring changes to the followers, the atmosphere, and the environment.

- A passionate leader has the energy and the drive to push and pull his team and organization to the next dimension.

- His passion is the source of energy that empowers followers, boosts personal efforts, and encourages team performance to reach higher levels. Matthew Arnold, poet and critic, once said, "Genius is merely an affair of energy, and some of the greatest transformations of our time were led by passionate leaders such as Bill Gates of Microsoft," not to mention Billy Graham. For several decades in the Twentieth Century, Billy

Graham was highly influential in bringing about transformation in the hearts and lives of many through the gospel of Christ.

"Passion, energy, enthusiasm, dedication, intensity, and zeal have always been the driving force of effective leaders."

As already mentioned, leadership is action, not position. Effective leaders initiate action that comes from energy, excitement, urgency, or a combination of these. This creates focus and harnesses the deep urge we all have to be part of something meaningful, knowing we are doing something important and striving for a worthy goal.

The passionate leader will stand and speak out for what he believes to inspire others, so that they are moved to follow and make a difference through his commitment to the outcome. His plan should be to help those he leads as follows:

1. Tap into and pursue their passion

2. Overturn their unbelief

3. Get rid of their anxiety

4. Unearth their convictions

5. Help them to be decisive in their actions

6. Manage their leadership weaknesses

7. Discover their leadership strengths

8. Determine their objectives

9. Strategize an action plan

10. Follow through to completion

9.5 Principle Number 5—Lead with Commitment

No effective spiritual leader can afford to underestimate the power of commitment. There's something compelling about being dedicated to a cause, committed to a vision, or pursuing a meaningful purpose, especially one God has called you to. It is one of the core concepts supporting the argument that leadership is not dependent on authority, rank, or label. It depends on whether the leader is wholly committed to what he or she believes is possible and prepared to live with whatever consequences it brings. If you can dream it, go ahead and pursue it. If you can see it, you can have it. Bravery produces competence, and responsibility takes precedence over domination.

The decision to act on what you have committed to and are passionate about will inevitably send you on a unique journey of discovery. Suddenly, you will become more aware of the events around you. You will also be more aware of opportunities. These are situations you would have previously ignored. It is like buying a particular model car, say a BMW, and suddenly seeing all the BMWs on the road. It's not that they weren't there before, but that you have only begun to notice them. The point is that until you are involved, there is hesitancy—a tendency to take a back seat and feel unequal to the task. But the moment you commit yourself, providence also begins to be activated. You will begin to see all manner of aid to assist you.

An unengaged leader is a danger to himself and his followers. When a follower is not committed because of limited influence, it may be of little consequence. But when a leader is uncommitted, he will not only fail himself and God but also bring failure to those he leads. **Zachariah 10: 1-3** says,

> "Ask the Lord for rain in the time of the latter rain. The Lord will make flashing clouds; He will give them showers of rain, grass in the field for everyone. For the idols speak delusion; the diviners envision lies, and tell false dreams, they comfort in vain. Therefore, the people went their way like sheep; they are in trouble because there is no shepherd. My anger is kindled against the shepherds, and I will punish the goatherds, for the Lord of Host will visit his flock, the House of Judah and will make them like His royal horse in the battle."

If you are going to conform to the dynamics of effective spiritual leadership, you will have to commit to the values inherent in your role: behavior, expectations, recognition, ownership, communication, courtesy, enthusiasm, and teamwork. Each leader must strive to live out those values. In fact, to become an effective leader, you must show your commitment to such goals by embracing the leadership code of ethics.

Effective leaders should promise to uphold these expectations so that they may know, own, energize, build, and promote an excellent spirit of sustainable growth and development. A good place to start is to;

    1. Show kindness to everyone you meet.

2. Be ready to give a word of encouragement to those in need.

3. Convey appreciation by saying "thank you," etc.

4. Offer verbal and written recognition for support received.

5. Promote good spiritual leadership outside of your church or organization, such as in your family, etc.

You have to believe that this commitment will help you live your vision to be an effective leader trusted to deliver anointed spiritual leadership to those you lead. You should make a pledge as follows. We, the leaders of (name your organization), make a personal and affirmative pledge to your thriving spiritual well-being, creating an ideal spiritual atmosphere in (name of your organization) as a demonstration of our commitment. As trusted spiritual leaders, we pledge to:-

- Focus on the following areas: spiritual quality of worship services, or quality of service provided if you are not a spiritual leader.

- Special and equal treatment of people irrespective of background, affluence, or social class.

- Pay special attention to visitors to ensure everyone's satisfactory level of growth and development and to show good stewardship in the area of finance.

- Compare results periodically (say monthly) on each of the above areas.

- Embrace the small but important necessities. For example,

thank-you notes, follow-up phone calls, etc.

- Pay special attention to leadership evaluation, identification, selection, appointment, and training of potential leaders, as an integral part of our operation.

- Sustain our leadership responsibility by holding ourselves and others accountable for achieving goals.

- Develop excellent leaders by providing ongoing coaching and mentoring, leadership development, and training at scheduled times.

- Allocate resources needed to succeed.

- Communicate effectively with all levels of the church or organization.

- Lead by positive example and learn from other successful leaders.

Your goal should be to create a culture that is ultimately focused on service, spirituality, and operational excellence. should pledge to create a place where the "so-called down and outs in society" are invited in to find love and comfort.

9.6 Principle Number 6—Lead with Confidence

An effective spiritual leader must be confident. One of the most profound statements of confidence recorded in the scriptures is found in **Job 3:15**. At the moment of grief and utter desperation, Job spoke these words, "Though He slays me, yet will I trust Him." For the unbeliever, this amounts to nothing but a fictitious story from a storybook. It confounds the wise, and yet it is the kind of affirmation that God uses to build His kingdom in our darkest hour.

This kind of statement disturbs the very foundations of hell; it upholds the whole concept of commitment and, even when faced with death, can undermine the confidence of a dynamic spiritual leader. To quote John Maxwell, "Why has terrorism, for instance, become such an international problem? Because terrorists have already given their lives for their cause? They will drive a truck full of explosives into enemy headquarters because they no longer hold their lives dear." This was precisely where Job was—living a life fully committed to God, even if it meant death. This is the place where we will find complete freedom—a place where no temptation, no threat, no bribe, and no sin or enticement can dissuade us from our commitment to God. This is summed up in **Galatians 2:20**: "I have been crucified with Christ; it is no longer I who live, but Christ who lives in me, and the life which I now live in the flesh, I live by faith in the Son of God, who loved me and gave Himself for me." It is here that God can really use us to accomplish great and mighty things for His glory and His kingdom.

9.7 Principle Number 7—Lead with Competence

Every effective spiritual leader must be competent. It's not that difficult for a charismatic individual to storm in and rise to the top, given the right conditions. But the question is, how do you stay at the top year in and year out? This has to be a question of competence.

There can be no substitute for the ability to perform. John F. Kennedy once said, "A rising tide lifts all boats." This describes the idea that when an organization performs well, everyone benefits. If, for example, your church is enjoying a revival and your followers' interest is high, it is easy for any leader to look capable. The real challenge will only appear in tough times, when it is necessary to make difficult decisions. Those who have the confidence to stay with the vision will shine in the darkest of times. Competence requires a leader to have the necessary tools for any occasion and to know when to use each one. This means the leader understands what is best in any situation, regardless of personal difficulties, because you choose to do what is to be done, and you are assured you can do all things through Christ who strengthens you. Competence also means having the confidence to admit mistakes and grow from them publicly and openly.

Competence does not come from observation and handing down orders to others. It's all about taking action. Doing what you know in your heart is the best thing to do, regardless of what lesser options are available. **2 Chronicles chapters 29 through 31** tell us that King Hezekiah took action when he came to the kingdom. The scripture says he did what was right in the sight of the Lord. He first cleansed the temple of its idol worshipping; then, he opened the door of the house of the Lord and repaired them. Then he restored temple worship, then he kept the Passover, and the Bible says in **2 Chronicles 31:21** ''And in every work that he began in the service of the house of God, in the law and in the commandments, to seek his God, he did it with all his heart, so he prospered. Competent leaders aren't looking for personal gain, but by simply taking action, you will reap prosperity. Neither do they focus on the rebellious negatives all leaders face. A competent leader sees the big picture and can deliver the right outcome at the right time. Competent leaders are not always celebrated because they aren't looking for praise and don't make the kind of mistakes that make headlines. But if you look at a well-run organization with a long history of success and a leader with a long track record, you will find a leader with vast confidence.

9.8 Principle Number 8—Lead by Taking Responsibility

An impactful spiritual leader is one who embraces responsibility wholeheartedly. They thrive on the challenges that come with leadership and find joy in guiding others. Their genuine appreciation for responsibility not only inspires those around them but also fosters trust and confidence in their vision.

The Merriam-Webster Dictionary defines responsibility as being "liable to be called to account."

As a church leader, you are ultimately responsible for everything that happens in your ministry. You will be held accountable for everything, whether good or bad. In order to take responsibility, you need to cross-examine the decisions and mechanisms that hold your ministry together. The consequences of not having this kind of awareness can be disastrous. The fact is it is not an excuse to say that you didn't know what was going on or you weren't personally involved—the responsibility is yours.

Inexperienced and newly appointed leaders are especially at risk of having their abilities tested in tough situations. If they inherit a defective system, they may not even realize it, partly because they may be inundated by the pressures of a new position and lack the knowledge to realize things are out of place. This is particularly true of new leaders promoted from within: they may be too shy to take the initiative to overturn decisions made by their former leaders, to whom they may feel they owe a certain degree of loyalty.

Taking full responsibility is an enormous challenge, and it can feel overwhelming. However, "leaders who plan for this responsibility right from the start (that is, when they accept the status of a leader) have a far greater chance of success than those who refuse to take responsibility."

So how, then, do you take responsibility? If you are going to fulfill your obligations as a leader and for everything that goes on within your organization, you need to develop a thorough understanding of the ministry's operating procedures. You can do this by re-examining your institution's aims. Of course, it will have a mission statement and other documents outlining its aims and objectives; you should look at these as your first step. It may be necessary to ponder over this mission statement and consider how faithfully it represents the purpose of your operation. Is it still correct, and will it likely motivate people to behave correctly? If you have doubts, then you need to clarify these, one way or another.

9.9 Principle Number 9—Must have a Teachable Spirit

It is important that spiritual leaders have a heart willing to learn and receive instruction. This will enable the leader to become wise and increase in knowledge and wisdom. (**Proverbs 9:9**) explains it like this.

"Give instruction to a wise man, and he will be still wiser; teach a just man, and he will increase in learning."

What then are the benefits of having a heart that is open to instruction? These are evidenced in the lives of many Bible characters in the Old and New Testaments. Let's look at a few, beginning with the characters used in our illustration of how God raised leaders.

9.9.1 Moses—A Meek Man with a Teachable Heart

"Now the man Moses was very humble (meek), above all the men who were upon the face of the earth." (**Numbers 12:3**).

Moses was a meek and humble man with a teachable spirit. At the start of his journey with God, the Lord promised he would be taught what to say and do. (**Exodus 4:12**) And God was faithful to lead Moses step by step throughout his journey, giving him instructions along the way. Moses was also highly motivated to learn from and lean on the Lord's guidance. When the Israelites became obstinate and unruly, or when Pharaoh proved stubborn, Moses would seek the Lord for further direction and encouragement. Moses's leadership style exemplified the need for leaders to be teachable, humble, and submissive to the Lord our God.

9.9.2 David – A Man Who Sought to Do God's Will

David, too, benefited from a heart open to instruction. In the Psalms, we read how David repeatedly called out to God, asking for His guidance and direction. Here are some verses that demonstrate David's disposition regarding his teachability. Read each verse and note the connection between being teachable and doing God's will.

- Show me your ways, O LORD; teach me your paths. (**Psalms 25:4**)

- Lead me in your truth, and teach me: for you are the God of my salvation; on you do I wait all the day. (**Psalms 25:5**)

- Teach me your way, O LORD, and lead me in a level path, because of my enemies. (**Psalms 27:11**)

- Teach me your way, O LORD; I will walk in your truth: unite my heart to fear your name. (**Psalms 86:11**)

- Teach me to do your will; for you are my God: your Spirit is good; lead me into the land of uprightness. (**Psalms 143:10**)

By studying these verses, you should have learnt of the relationship between being teachable and following God. In this regard, you are to pray for God to teach you, and you must accompany your prayer requests with a heart and desire to do His will. As you seek to know God's will, you must understand that the process of discerning God's will for your life requires you to learn from Him.

9.9.3 Jesus – The Greatest Example of a Teachable Spirit

And the Child grew and became strong in spirit, filled with wisdom; and the grace of God was upon Him. (**Luke 2:40**)

No one demonstrated learning God's will by being teachable, as Jesus did. Just take a look at his responsibility for a moment. He left the splendor of heaven, born into a world full of sin, yet He had the challenge of living a faultless life even unto the death of the cross. For that reason, Jesus lived very near to His Father, seeking His will and being ever sensitive to His guidance.

"Then Jesus answered and said to them, 'Most assuredly, I say to you, the Son can do nothing of Himself, but what He sees the Father do: for whatsoever things He does, these also do the Son likewise." **(John 5:19)**

Jesus showed us that our ultimate teacher is not man but God our Father. By giving us the Holy Spirit, the Father has enabled us to listen to Him and learn to follow his leading. "But the Comforter, who is the Holy Spirit, whom the Father will send in my name, he shall teach you all things, and bring all things to your remembrance, whatever I have said unto you." **(John 14:26)**

9.9.4 The Apostles – Led by the Holy Spirit

''But you will receive power when the Holy Spirit has come upon you. You will be witnesses to me in Jerusalem, in all Judea and Samaria, and to the uttermost parts of the earth." **(Acts 1:8)**

Jesus instructed the Apostles and first disciples not to proceed with their mission of saving the world without the power of the Holy Spirit. As we read through the Book of Acts, we see how the Holy Spirit empowered and instructed the disciples on how they should go. "When they had gone through the region of Phrygia and Galatia, they were forbidden by the Holy Spirit to speak the word in Asia. When they had come opposite Mysia, they tried to go into Bithynia, but the Spirit didn't allow them." (**Acts 16:6-7**)

For us human beings, it is much easier to try to do God's will in our own wisdom and strength. But we should do all we can to resist such temptation. Instead of trying to figure things out in our heads, we should seek to become more familiar with the Spirit of God's leading in a more intimate way, so we can learn to hear His voice and follow His leading. This approach will lead us to greater leadership success.

9.9.5 God's Word – Written for Our Instruction Today

"All scripture is given by inspiration of God, and is profitable for doctrine, for reproof, for correction, and for instruction in righteousness." (**2 Timothy 3:16**)

As believers today, we are so fortunate to have the Spirit of God living within us and the Word of God to guide us. God's Word reveals to us the way of salvation so we can come to know the Lord. (**2 Timothy 3:15**) It also teaches us how we should live and conduct ourselves in this world. The Word of God is indeed a "lamp unto our feet and a light unto our path." (**Psalm 119:105**) God's Word gives us discernment and helps us to grow and mature. (**Hebrews 5:12-14**) Spending time in God's Word is essential to our growth in Christ. But simply reading the Bible will not do the trick. We must approach God's Word with a teachable heart and a willing spirit. "Open my eyes, that I may behold wondrous things out of your law." (**Psalms 119:18**) We must listen to how God speaks to our hearts through His Word and then act on what He teaches us. (**Matthew 11:15, James 1:22**) Life becomes exciting when we quiet our hearts and listen to our Father's whisper. **(Isaiah 30:21)** Open your heart to the Lord today and ask him in sincerity, "Lord, teach me Your ways."

Adapted from www.christian

growth network.com/ teachablespirit.html

I am well aware of the challenges associated with a leadership persona that does not proudly vaunt itself. Some will take that as a sign of weakness, but you must understand that, despite the opinions of others, you must be teachable. Here is why: if you want to understand the church's successes and failures, listen to people's conversations wherever they meet. Church politics can often consume excessive time and resources. Unhealthy gossip is also a distraction from work and demoralizes the workers. It is much more productive to spend more time in the Word, listen to God's voice, and follow instructions.

9.10 Principle Number 10—Lead Without Exploitation

Servant leaders do not exploit; please do not be tempted. This is never a good practice. In fact, it can be one of the most destructive elements of an organization and is often the enemy within.

In the first few chapters of the Book of Nehemiah, we see that the work is threatened by external enemies such as Sanballat and Tobiah. However, in Chapter 5, we find that the real enemy was among the workers. It occurred because, while they worked to rebuild Jerusalem's wall, they neglected their crops, resulting in famine. Desperate to obtain food, many were forced to mortgage their fields, their vineyards, their homes, and even their brothers as slaves. It was a dire situation that, in some cases, led to homelessness. Many sold their possessions while others borrowed money from their Jewish brothers to pay their taxes, which only plunged them further into debt. This situation was further heightened by exploitation due to the high interest rates Israelites charged their fellow Hebrews on such loans. But Nehemiah and some others had redeemed (repurchased) Hebrews who had been sold as slaves to foreigners. **(See Neh. 5:8)** Others had done the opposite by selling their sons and daughters into slavery to survive.

Nehemiah was greatly displeased; he was indignant about the selfishness and greed of those exploiting others for personal gain. He dealt with the issue head-on and in the face of opposition. He offered a harsh rebuke and asked the exploiters to stop the exploitation and restore their possessions to the people. He helped the needy by lending money and grain without interest (**Nehemiah 5:10, 14-15**).

Note how the people responded! They responded by agreeing to forgive the debts, saying, "We will do what you say" (**v.12**). If you are a leader who has used exploitation and manipulation for selfish gains, please reconsider your position and restore to the people of God whatever you have taken unjustifiably.

Do you remember what Zacchaeus did following his encounter with Jesus? First, he offered to give half of his goods to the poor, and secondly, he said that if he had taken anything from anyone by false accusations/exploitation, he would restore four times the amount, **Luke 19:1-10.** Notice, no one told him to do so; his conscience did. In our generation, however, some have no conscience when exploiting others for selfish ambitions, so be warned.

Nehemiah held the highest position in the nation at the time: governor. Despite his high position, he demonstrated principles of good leadership. Let's examine them here.

Nehemiah never took advantage of his position (**V14-15**). His position gave him the right to feed and entertain the officials under him at the government's expense, but he chose not to use this option. He was also able to impose very high taxes, but he refused.

Nehemiah was very hands-on and shared the workload. (**v. 16a**) Many leaders hand down orders from a distance, never getting their hands dirty, which pretty much explains the performance style of secular management, as I explained at the beginning of this chapter—but please note that Nehemiah applied himself to work in the same way as Jesus modeled servanthood. I refer to this as "leading from the front" by self-application. This is one of the hallmarks of a good leader, someone who has no problem getting down and dirty—by showing exactly how it is done. Spiritual leaders do not take unfair advantage of the situation, and neither did Nehemiah. (**v. 16b**) "Just like the stock market's version of insider trading, Nehemiah had opportunities to make more money by purchasing land under the table, but he didn't do that." Once again, your position as a leader does not give you the right to take advantage and exploit others for selfish ambition. Great spiritual leaders committed their resources, and so did Nehemiah (**v .16c-18**). Nehemiah committed his servants (**v. 16**), his table to feed others (**v. 17**), and his wealth (**v. 17-18**).

He showed great compassion for the people he led (**v. 15-18**). Nehemiah knew the situation, felt the pain, understood the people's plight, and carried the heavy burden of the people, refusing to increase taxes as his predecessors had done.

Probably more importantly, Nehemiah, like any good spiritual leader, prayed and trusted God with confidence and a clear conscience (**v. 19**). "Remember me, God, for good, according to all I have done for this people," he prayed.

It is likely that you can identify with the Hebrews, who were oppressed by enemies such as hunger, mortgage debt they could not repay, and high interest rates. Perhaps you are a leader who is guilty of burdening the poor through oppression rather than through relief and compassion. God loves a cheerful giver and demands that we act compassionately, primarily for the poor. We must follow the example of Nehemiah and the apostles to reflect God's love in our actions toward others. (**See 2 Thess. 3:7-15.**)

9.11 Principle Number 11—Find a Need and Fill It

In my book entitled 'Mastering the Art of Personal Evangelism,' I delve into the powerful principle of "find a need and fill it." This concept stands out as one of the most compelling strategies for effectively sharing the gospel. By identifying others' genuine needs and addressing them with compassion and understanding, we can create meaningful connections that open the door to spiritual conversations and growth.

This also applies to effective leadership, and I have found it to be one of the most fundamental business principles. It is said that, in the 1800s, a Vermont blacksmith became known for his reliable, sturdy workmanship. When words came from the West of vast fields capable of growing produce far more than what Vermont could grow, hundreds of people migrated there. This blacksmith went with them and soon detected a severe problem. The cast-iron plows the pioneers took from the East didn't work well in the Midwest. The rich Midwestern soil stuck to them, so they had to make frequent stops to scrape it from the plow with every few steps. In 1837, through trial and error, the blacksmith designed a plow from a discarded sawmill blade. It was a polished plow that cleaned itself as it plowed. He built and sold ten of them and then received orders for many more. As he manufactured these plows, he kept changing them, causing some to criticize him. But he replied, "If we don't improve our product, somebody else will." By 1836, he produced 13,000 plows a year and became the largest plow manufacturer in the United States. This man just saw a need and filled it. The same principle is true from a spiritual point of view. Sometimes we feel like giving up because of the immoral conditions of our day, but you must remember this first principle of leadership: Good leadership meets the needs of the hour.

You may say you do not know where to begin, but that's precisely the problem. If you have no sense of purpose, vision, or direction, why would anyone choose to follow you? Think about it, if you were not the leader, would you want to follow someone like you? You may not only have no sense of direction or purpose, but you may not possess the drive, determination, and will to transform the world around you for good. For example, you may ask, "Where can I find a need to fill?" You do not have to look very far. There are needs in your local prison, homeless shelters, on the streets, among drug addicts, and alcohol abusers. There is a desperate need around us. Some are turning to drugs and soothsayers because we are not available. Many of us are far too busy building our empires when there are souls to rescue. Don't you know that if you can give hope to someone, they will be willing to follow you and tell their friends about you and your ministry? I can guarantee you they will.

Chapter Checklist

In Review

- Success will not come if you wait on some other person or some other time.

- Discouragement and failure are stepping stones to success.

- Successful spiritual leaders lead and not manage.

- Successful spiritual leaders lead by building effective relationships.

- Successful spiritual leaders lead with discernment.

- Successful spiritual leaders lead with passion.

- Successful spiritual lead with commitment.

- Successful spiritual leaders lead with confidence.

- Successful spiritual leaders lead with competence.

- Successful spiritual leaders lead by taking responsibility.

- Successful spiritual leaders are teachable.

- Successful spiritual leaders lead and don't exploit.

Personal Notes

Chapter Ten
MAKING IT HAPPEN/SOME PROTOCOLS

10.1 Understand Your Mission—Know Your Goals

Many leaders have found success simply by following God's design plan and purpose for their lives. There is a specific task God has called each of us, and if you are trying to operate outside the boundaries of your calling, there is a very high chance you will fail. There may be several reasons for this, but the most significant is that you are operating outside your comfort zone. In fact, it may be okay to operate outside your comfort zone, but if this takes you outside God's design plan and purpose for your life, you are heading for trouble. It is therefore imperative that you have a full appreciation of the purpose for which you have been called, for instance;

If you have been called to the ministry of evangelism, you need to understand the objective of sharing the gospel. For example, you need to know what you want to achieve, your goals, and your target audience. If you do not understand what you are trying to achieve, you will certainly achieve nothing. Even Jesus did not doubt His mission. Listen to what He said when He quoted Isaiah in **Luke 4:18-19.** "The Spirit of the Lord *is* upon Me because He has anointed Me to preach the gospel to *the* poor; He has sent Me to heal the broken-hearted, to proclaim liberty to *the* captives and recovery of sight to *the* blind, t*o* set at liberty those who are oppressed; to proclaim the acceptable year of the Lord."

As you can see, Jesus clearly understood His mission. And if Jesus needed to know why He was sent, how about you and I? If God has called you, He has called you to something unique and original. Whatever He called you to do is unique and embedded in your DNA. After all, he is the creative genius who does not need to clone anyone, and neither does He make copies. Everything God creates is original. That's why your fingerprints are yours alone.

Now, when I refer to the gifting and calling of God on one's life, I'm not referring to a vague desire or good idea. I'm talking about motivation so strong that you cannot find peace until you are in your rightful place. This desire will consume your every thought—it is something so intense that it wakes you in the middle of the night, burning deep within you—a fire that will not go out.

I have seen many church leaders go about their business as though they had no real purpose, just meeting and holding services. Many do not even want to reach out to their local community. Why? because they have no fire burning deep within and no conviction of the message they have to share. Their congregations only grow because of church hoppers, not new converts.

The church hoppers wander from one place to another, seeking the perfect church. Unstable as water, they can neither excel nor help you to excel. They are of little help as you try to build a successful ministry. They will come for a while, but eventually do what they do best—move on. Instability does not lend itself to success because it is unreliable and useless in any context.

After fully appreciating your mission, your next step toward becoming a successful spiritual leader is to implement and follow basic yet essential protocols for your ministry.

10.2 First Impression

Your primary aim must be to create a positive and lasting first impression. You know what they say about first impressions, right? They always leave an indelible imprint on the heart and mind of the recipient. In the case of a church, and as already mentioned in the introductory chapter, paragraph seven, the first person a visitor is likely to encounter is the person at the door—be it the usher or a greeter, as the case may be. The reception your first-time visitors receive will determine (1) whether they listen to and hear your message or (2) whether they will return to your church. It means that from day one, training and development are paramount and crucial to your ministry's success. The emphasis here is foundation; the foundation you lay will determine the kind of structure you build. Many leaders seem to believe it is acceptable to adopt a laid-back approach, thinking they will make the necessary changes as and when required, but that will almost certainly be disastrous and further complicate things in the long run. The principle here is to **get it right the first time**. If this is not how you have been thinking, do yourself a favor and please reconsider. "Practice makes perfect." All personnel should be well trained: ushers, altar workers, greeters, moderators, etc.; whatever we do for God should be done with a spirit of excellence.

From day one, training and development are paramount and therefore crucial to the success of your ministry.

I believe these personnel (especially ushers and greeters) should not only be taught interpersonal skills but also encouraged to feel free to inform the leadership of any reason that may affect their performance while on duty. For instance, if an usher or greeter had an awkward moment with their husband or wife on Saturday night and felt down Sunday morning, it would be a good idea to excuse them from their duties, as it could negatively affect their ability to perform effectively.

10.3 Presentation

Whenever I enter a church for the first time, the first thing I notice is the sanctuary's presentation. I will immediately scan the surroundings, and quite frankly, sometimes, I am astounded by what I see. You do not have to wait for the president or the queen to visit before you take the time and effort to make the place of worship a pleasant one. Sometimes, all that is needed is a bucket of paint and a few volunteers one morning to transform the place. Remember, you are accommodating the Holy Spirit, the supreme ruler of heaven and earth. Besides, it would be best if you made it a pleasant place for the senior citizen walking with the aid of a walking stick. They, too, deserve to have a pleasant place for worship.

Sometimes, you do not realize that a member of yours, who is— say, a nurse, may have a doctor colleague they would like to invite to your church, but is reluctant because of the state of your place of worship. It doesn't have to be this way; put your best foot forward. You are a child of a king, and therefore, your surroundings must bear the hallmark of royalty, so to speak.

10.4 Worship Team

Worship is the heartbeat of the church; you can visit any successful ministry and immediately notice that it has a strong worship team. Worship is not just about singing it is about ushering in the presence of the Lord into your midst. When the presence of the Lord is in the house, anything can happen. You will experience healing and deliverance, and the power of God will transform lives. After all, "It is the anointing that destroys the yoke."(**Isaiah 10:27**) It is the anointing that makes preaching flow and brings the Word to life. Anointed worship creates a pleasant atmosphere for even the unsaved. Trust me on this: get your worship up to standard, and visitors will keep returning for more. To reiterate, the effective leader will ensure that the worship team consists of people with not merely great singing voices. They will seek out those who are committed to a lifestyle of worship. In other words, they are not people who come to perform or those who come in fulfillment of their moral duties in the church. They are people who spend time in the presence of the Lord, even outside the four walls of the Church building.

1. The leader must ensure that the worship team meets for prayer and consecration.

2. It is the leader's responsibility to ensure that a suitable and convenient place is set aside for the worship team to carry out their rehearsals. All professional singers know the importance of spending quality time in rehearsal to get it right, so why shouldn't you? I grew up in the church in the nineteen seventies and sang in a group called the "Action Melodeons." And although we were extremely popular in and around our local communities at that time, to be perfectly honest, we failed to take rehearsal seriously. There were times when we were not even aware of the songs we would be singing that night until we actually arrived on stage. This kind of approach is not good enough.

3. Worship should include offering the highest respect to the Holy Spirit so that He is well-accommodated and free to do what He pleases.

In a church where the worship team is not the same as the choir, I would recommend that the worship team sit together in the front row and be readily available at all times. The team must also be alert and ready to minister at the end of the message. I have been to many churches where the worship team simply returns to their seats throughout the building after the worship session and has no further active role in the service. I believe one of the most crucial aspects of the service is ministering to the needs of those who follow the message.

I am aware that not many of our churches pay attention to this aspect of the service; however, this is where it all happens. "God inhabits the praises of His people." (**Psalm 22:3**). Therefore, the worship team has a vital role to play here. What's the point of preaching a powerful sermon only to send people home sick, broke, busted, and disgusted, facing the same old problems week in and week out? To ensure that's not the case, you should make a concerted effort to minister to people's needs. This is what it means to be a minister. A pivotal part of Jesus's ministry was meeting people's needs, not just their spiritual needs. Consider this: to the hungry, the gospel is all about food. Until those needs are met, they have little use for the gospel. Jesus would heal the sick, raise the dead, unplug deaf ears, open the eyes of the blind, and would typically complete the process by declaring, "Your faith has made you whole,"—not just made you well but entirely whole—body, soul, and spirit.

One reason some preachers do not minister to people's needs in this way is that they do not believe they have the gift for it. But let's face it! If God has called you to minister the word, you must minister to the needs of the people. The problem is that most preachers get too preoccupied with immediate results. But that is not your business; do what God has called you to do, and leave the rest to Him. Remember these words, "Paul planted, Apollos watered, and God gave the increase." (**1 Corinthians 3:6**) If the worship team maintains a level of anointing during the ministry at the altar, you can rest assured you will soon be hearing testimonies of healing and deliverance. Practice makes perfect, but whatever you do, please do not force anything on anyone or try to impress. God does not operate this way and will not honor such practices. Again, you are not fulfilling the call of God on your life. If you deliver an impactful message, but then send the people of God home unchanged, you may undermine that message. Some churches make an effort to conclude with prayer, but I often notice that even when a service is excellent, there is insufficient time scheduled for ministry at the end. This leaves God's work unresolved and may frustrate the Holy Spirit, whose role is to complete that work. I'm not suggesting that the Holy Spirit can be disheartened, but it's important to ensure that ministry is prioritized.

10.5 Altar Workers

In addition to the roles of the worship team and the minister, every church should have specially trained people to minister to those at the altar. Call them what you wish, but I refer to them as ministers or altar workers. They should be trained to help lead people to Christ or minister to people's immediate needs.

Not long ago, I was at a meeting where I noticed some things that were out of place. First, I was laying hands on people [and let me pause here to say I am well aware that some of you may not be comfortable with practices like that and may even have your own opinion], but please do not be overly critical of something you do not fully understand or appreciate. This kind of practice is 100 percent biblical; let God be the judge. And then there are those who are overly zealous about such an operation, literally pushing people to the floor to prove a point.

If you are involved in such practices, please do not engage in them. God does not need your help, and you do not need to prove anything to anyone. The point I was making is that as I laid hands, the spirit slew one person and fell to the floor. To my amazement, no one was available to assist that individual. One explanation is that it may have been an unusual occurrence in that church, but it should never have happened. Trained personnel should have been on duty and ready to assist in such circumstances. In my next observation, I noticed that a lady needed assistance and was attended to by two male individuals. It may be more appropriate for female altar workers or ministers to assist women in these situations, encouraging a more supportive environment that aligns with acceptable practices.

The altar is where God does business in people's hearts, and it should be exceptionally welcoming, warm, and safe because our God loves needy people and wants them to encounter Him in various ways. Therefore, we dare not neglect a thing so important to God; we must take seriously the needs He wants to meet. Doing that will please God more than anything else we can do and make it a pleasant experience for all concerned.

Now that you have created a pleasant place for worship, i.e., the sanctuary, and selected your ushers, worshippers, and altar workers, you must bring order to the house of God. The atmosphere should now be set for you to feel comfortable inviting the Spirit of God, the president, and even the queen at short notice. At this point, you can rest assured that your members will not be inhibited when inviting their friends, family, and colleagues to church.

Probably the most critical thing absent from this equation is the leader himself. As a leader, you need to be fully committed to your vision, so it becomes your top priority. I do not believe that ministers should go to work outside the church, except it absolutely has to be and for a short time. If God has called you, your life and future are under His control. **2 Timothy 2:4** says: "No man engaged in this warfare entangles himself in the affairs of this life." And **Mathew 6:25-34** tells us:

"Therefore, I say to you, do not worry about your life, what you will eat or what you will drink; or about your body, what you will put on. Isn't life more than food and the body more than clothing? Look at the birds of the air, for they neither sow nor reap nor gather into barns; yet your heavenly Father feeds them. Are you not of more value than they? Which of you, by worrying, can add one cubit to his stature? "So why do you worry about clothing? Consider the lilies of the field, how they grow: they neither toil nor spin; and yet I say to you that even Solomon in all his glory was not arrayed like one of these. Now if God so clothes the grass of the field, which today is, and things the Gentiles seek. For your heavenly Father knows that you need all these things. But seek first the kingdom of God and His righteousness, and all these things shall be added to you. Therefore, do not worry about tomorrow, for tomorrow will worry about its own things. Sufficient for the day is its own trouble." tomorrow is thrown into the oven, will He not much more clothe you, O you of little faith? "Therefore, do not worry, saying, 'What shall we eat?' or 'What shall we drink?' or 'What shall we wear?' For after all these things the Gentiles seek. For your heavenly Father knows that you need all these things. But seek first the kingdom of God and His righteousness, and all these things shall be added to you. Therefore, do not worry about tomorrow, for tomorrow will worry about its own things. Sufficient for the day is its own trouble."

I recognize this is a particularly contentious topic, and I know many of you may need to maintain a secular job at various stages of your lives. However, to be an impactful leader in ministry, you must dedicate significant time to cultivating a deep relationship with the Lord. This means immersing yourself in prayer and reflection, exploring the Scriptures to gain insight and wisdom, and actively listening to and addressing the needs of those you are called to lead. Only by doing so can you truly embody the compassion and guidance that effective ministry requires.

10.6 Directives for Visiting Ministers

I cannot overstate the importance of providing clear, complete instructions to visiting speakers. It makes you look very professional, and failure to do so only invites problems and is likely to negatively affect the service's outcome.

Time and again, I have gone to minister at churches where the minister said nothing about how long I was expected to speak. This is important to me for several reasons. For example, as a matter of principle, I like to sing (worship) before I minister, which can take some time, and, of course, I like to leave time at the end for ministry. Many meetings I have attended are held in rented buildings. This usually reflects time constraints, yet the host pastor does not consider it important to inform the visiting minister that they must be out by a certain time. In fact, this information should be provided at the time of the invitation. This allows the visiting minister to consider the time factor in his final preparation. If this is not done, it could have unpleasant consequences for all. For instance, the host will likely become distracted and preoccupied with the potential consequences. The regular members are likely to become unsettled because it is common practice to get home at a set time, and the guest preacher may become rattled by the unrest.

These are all important attributes that give order to your ministry and make you look both ready and serious about doing business for God. Everyone around you will begin to feel the energy and start gearing up to work with you and help you to reach your goals.

10.7 Promoting the Vision

Having followed the above protocols, you are almost certainly ready for explosive growth in your ministry. At this point, I hope you are in ministry not only because you can preach a sermon, but also because you have been called by God and have a vision. Remember that you are leading because you have either been there or you know how to get there. Your duty is to plan the journey and lead from the front. To do so, you must not only have a vision but also communicate it and keep it fresh and up to date. This means you need to revisit your vision regularly. It would also help to have your vision statement posted on your wall/bulletin board for all to see. Your people need to be reminded where they are going and how to get there. In fact, you are probably wasting your time holding meetings week in and week out if very little is being done to promote the vision.

You are likely to have a wide range of talents, gifts, and professionals in your church. So whatever you do for God, do it with a spirit of excellence, thereby representing God with distinction. Remember, even if you are not educated, you have been called by God, and the office you hold is a very distinguished one, which means you have the right to be confident and, therefore, should never allow anyone to intimidate you for any reason.

The primary purpose and ultimate goal of every leader should not only be to develop followers but to develop leaders. Author and teacher John Maxwell once said, "Leaders who develop followers grow their organization, but only one person at a time, but leaders who develop leaders multiply their growth. This is because all the leaders they develop will also inherit that leader's followers. Add ten followers to your organization, and you have the power of ten leaders, each influencing all their followers. That's the difference between addition and multiplication. It's like growing your organization by teams instead of by individuals."

10.8 Interpersonal Skills

A true leader has strong interpersonal skills that draw people in. He also embraces diversity by allowing followers to disagree with him. Where would leaders be if there were no followers? Who would the teachers teach if there were no students?

Investopedia describes interpersonal skills as "the skills a person uses to interact with others properly. In business, the term generally refers to an employee's ability to work effectively with others while getting the job done. Interpersonal skills encompass communication, listening, attitude, and deportment. Good interpersonal skills are a prerequisite for numerous positions in many organizations."

Investopedia explains that the term "interpersonal skills" is ''somewhat of a misnomer because it refers to character traits possessed by an individual rather than skills that can be taught in the classroom. Within an organization, employees with good interpersonal skills are likely to be more productive than those with poor interpersonal skills because of their propensity to project a positive attitude and look for solutions to problems."

Good interpersonal skills are vital for nurturing and sustaining healthy relationships with others. These skills not only facilitate smooth communication and understanding but also play a key role in boosting your self-esteem. When you build strong connections with people, you often find yourself surrounded by individuals you admire and look up to, which can inspire personal growth. Enhancing your interpersonal skills allows you to build deeper, more meaningful connections with others. This journey not only enriches your relationships but also empowers you to engage more effectively with those around you.

10.9 Association Partnership

An association partnership is an agreement between two or more individuals to support one another. Every spiritual leader should develop meaningful "association partnerships." You might have heard the old idiom: "Two heads are better than one." If you learn to associate with others and build partnerships wherever you go, you increase the chances of multiplying your resources and extending your reach. Associating with like-minded individuals and building alliances will help you generate more ideas and achieve your goals.

As with all human beings, your followers expect to be appreciated for their efforts—it reassures them that you value their work and allows more room for creativity and improvement. A pat on the back, a congratulatory remark, or a handshake makes others feel appreciated and valued.

Every now and again, the people you lead may need a little motivation and encouragement to continue performing at their best. Routine can be tedious, lead to boredom, and prevent progress.

Mentoring, support, enabling, and advice are necessary to encourage your people to become better performers. A good leader understands that sharing his wisdom with his followers is one of the keys to both his success and theirs. Leadership is not just about personal growth. It's also about helping others grow to realize their full potential.

A good leader must learn to genuinely care for their followers and those around them. He shows empathy and sincerity and ultimately understands that each life is valuable to God.

Every good leader, particularly the spiritual leader, should be able to create instant rapport with others. They should have a natural inclination to interact and offer help to people from all walks of life. They understand that by helping others, they are unintentionally contributing to their success.

Once again, may I remind you that leadership is not about managing people—it's not about slavery! It's about liberating people from slavery so that they might realize their full potential. By replicating yourself, you empower others, which in turn enables you to accomplish far more and contribute to the broader growth of your organization and the community at large.

The challenge for every leader is to "swim against the tide," embrace cross-cultural ministry, and "become all things to all people, to win some." In other words, leaders will be successful if they are unafraid to challenge prevailing opinions, races, and cultures to reach everyone, wherever they are. All leaders must be ready to impact and transform the lives of those in their local ministries and communities, as well as those with whom they interact. This is not simply about getting along and conducting business as usual. It's past time for leaders in the Body of Christ to play catch-up; it's now time to lead so others can follow.

We must understand that culture is the unavoidable context of ministry, and to have maximum impact, we must understand the time and culture in which we live.

Leadership is the ability to motivate others to get things done. The leader has the personality and interpersonal skills to motivate others and help them achieve their goals; people love to follow a good leader. Following what you believe is right isn't always easy, especially when others don't share your view. This is one area where you may need to step outside your comfort zone to follow the path you know is right. You must be comfortable in your skin, especially when thinking for yourself. That encapsulates the telltale signs of a good leader.

10.10 Leaders Accept Others Where They Are

It is indispensable not to be judgmental in any shape or form. Jesus did not come to call the righteous but to call sinners to repentance. You should be willing and ready to accept everyone, irrespective of their appearance or lifestyle choices. Once again, observe how Jesus addressed the woman at the well's lifestyle. "Jesus told her, 'Go call your husband, and come here.'. The woman answered and said, 'I have no husband.' Jesus said to her, 'You have well said I have no husband, for you have had five husbands, and the one whom you now have is not your husband; in that you spoke truly.'" **(John 4:16-18)**

Her lifestyle was now out in the open, and yet Jesus did not condemn her for it. Your duty is to restore and renew, not to pass judgment on anyone.

10.11 Leaders Should Stick with Real Issues

Navigating this situation can be quite complex, as it's important to avoid coming across as a dictator or being perceived as excessively controlling. Nonetheless, a truly effective leader often needs to take the initiative, particularly when engaging in critical discussions that require a focus on underlying issues. This balance between assertiveness and approachability is essential for fostering a constructive dialogue while ensuring that important matters are addressed head-on. That's because you cannot allow others to derail your vision. In other words, you must not be drawn away from the key issues. In my book, **"Mastering the Art of Personal Evangelism," I explained that when sharing the gospel, you cannot allow others to dictate the terms and conditions of the discussion.** Notice this illustration in **John 4:19-24**:

> *"The woman said to Him, 'Sir, I perceive that you are a prophet. Our fathers worshipped on this mountain, and you Jews say Jerusalem is the place where one ought to worship.' Jesus said to her, 'Woman, believe me, the hour is coming when you will neither on this mountain nor in Jerusalem worship the Father. You worship what you do not know; we know what we worship, for salvation is of the Jews. But the hour is coming, and now is, when the true worshippers will worship the Father in spirit and in truth, for the Father is*

seeking such to worship him. God is a spirit, and they that worship Him must worship Him in spirit and in truth.'"

So, yes, Jesus took control of the conversation and stayed focused on the key issues to get His message across.

10.12 Leaders Communicate Issues Directly and Simply (John 4:25-26)

"The woman said to Him, "I know that Messiah is coming" (who is called Christ). "When He comes, He will tell us all things. "Jesus said to her, 'I who speak to you am *He*."

Observe how Jesus, with a sense of ease and grace, unveiled His identity as the Messiah. In that moment, He tenderly offered her the ultimate gift: the water of life, a transformative blessing that only He could provide. His words flowed naturally, reflecting both His divine authority and His deep compassion, inviting her to quench her spiritual thirst in a way that was both profound and straightforward.

Chapter Checklist

In Review

- Many leaders found success by following God's pattern (**Exodus 25:40**)

- There is a special task God has called each of us to fulfill.

- Operating outside your calling could prove catastrophic.

- You must understand your mission.
- You must create a good first impression.
- **Workers** must be adequately trained
- Establish an order for visiting ministers.
- You must promote your vision.
- You must develop good interpersonal skills.
- Leaders accept others where they are.
- Leaders should stick to real issues.
- Leaders should communicate issues directly and simply.

Personal Notes

_____

_____

_____

_____

_____

_____

Chapter Eleven
SUMMARY AND BASIC RULES NOT TO IGNORE

Basic Rules of Leadership

Many people have good intentions, but do not always act as intended. As Vince Lombardi once said, "the will to win means nothing without the will to prepare. This is especially true for leaders. Most leaders start well and with good intentions, but many stray from the blueprint that would assure their success. Many meet with their congregation week in, week out and hold meetings, but with little sense of purpose. They have no strategy, no vision, and no clear objectives. It was Zig Ziglar who once made this seemingly ironic yet profound statement: "If you aim at nothing, you'll hit it every time." Nothing could be more accurate than this: if you do not know what you are aiming to achieve, you will, without fail, accomplish nothing.

One thing is clear: when these leaders meet with their congregations, they usually have fantastic programs so well-planned that, sadly, even the Holy Spirit has trouble getting past their front doors. So what, then, is the problem? The problem is that the fundamental leadership rules are often missing from the equation. But to achieve authentic success and be an effective leader, you must take consistent action. This means you must be consistent in applying all the basic rules of leadership. Let's look at a summary of these basic yet all-important rules not to be missed.

- **Goal Setting** — All leaders should set goals greater than those they have achieved in the past. It would help if you always planned for the future while making sure that the people you lead have the capacity to rise to the occasion.

- **Attitude of the Leader** — The leader's attitude must be exemplary. For example, the leader must always be optimistic and focus on solutions rather than problems.

- **An Effective Leader must be Responsible**. — It is vitally important that the leader takes responsibility and quickly admits mistakes. As a leader, you are responsible for what goes wrong in your organization, so the buck stops with you.

- **Must be Decisive** — No leader will make the right decision every time, but all decisions should be made decisively and for the right reasons. Then even if not all of them are right, most will be wise.

- **Must Seek God's Guidance** — Never forget to seek God's guidance, strive to do the right thing, and leave the outcome to Him.

- **Must Put Others First** — Successful leaders always put others before themselves. I can guarantee that when the people you lead see that you have their best interests at heart, they will work harder to please you. When they realize that their success is your goal, they will cease to care how much you know, to know how much you care!

- **Must Set a Good Example** – A good leader should lead by example. Please remember that leading is not the same as management, although they are complementary. A good leader does not just tell others what to do; they lead from the front, showing them how it is done. You must take the lead by setting the right example for your team.

- **Must be Committed** – Every effective leader must demonstrate a profound commitment to integrity and strong character. It is crucial that your integrity remains beyond reproach, as any doubt can undermine your authority. When your followers see you consistently make ethical decisions and do what is right, they will develop trust and confidence in your leadership. This trust fosters a culture of respect and loyalty, enabling a more cohesive and motivated team.

- **Must Always Strive for Excellence** – Every leader should strive for excellence in every area and at all times. Excellence in attitude, appearance, work ethic, and dedication will go a long way toward success.

- **Must Aim for Improved Personal Growth and Development** – Being a leader should be a lifelong learning experience. In other words, you are to be a student for life. Leaders must be committed to their personal growth and development. People will be much more likely to follow you if you make it a point of duty to advance your skills at all times.

- **Must be persistent and Determined** — Every leader must demonstrate persistence and determination. Genuine success takes time to achieve. The big question is, how much time? And the answer is, as long as it takes! These rules are essential to a leader's success. Ignore them at your peril.

The fundamental question is: What does effective leadership depend on? Here's a summary.

- **Must have Excellent Communication and Interpersonal Skills** - Effective communication is critical to any leader who wants to get their point across. If your followers have no clear idea what to do or how to do it, how can they succeed?

- **Must be motivated** - Successful leaders are motivated individuals who are also gifted at motivating their people. If followers are not adequately motivated, they will become stagnant. To increase motivation, challenge your followers with goals that may be outside their comfort zone.

- **Must Always Encourage Teamwork** - This is not just about teaching your people to work together; you should also be part of the team. To become a better leader, recognize others' gifts and skills and enable them to use them.

- **Must have a Mentor**—Take the time to learn everything you can about leadership, especially spiritual leadership. Make sure you have a mentor you can contact for guidance.

It has been said, "Leadership has not been tried and found difficult, but instead has been found difficult and left largely untried." (**Author unknown**)

- **Never use your Mouth to kill your Dreams** – Please remember that, whatever you do, you must maintain a positive attitude, especially when things do not appear promising. I'm sure you have heard people say, "I would rather have five good people in my organization than 100 bad ones." Not me. I would rather have 100 wayward individuals to demonstrate that I have the leadership skills to turn them around than have five self-righteous individuals to manage. Please be careful what you say, as you might get what you ask for.

- There's only one way to succeed in anything, and that is to give it everything, and the quality of a man's life is in direct proportion to his commitment to excellence, regardless of his chosen field of endeavor, Vince Lombardi

In Summary:

Effective leadership is not an unreachable dream. However, it takes thought, preparation, and a heart willing to move with the Spirit of God when He says to move. As leaders, it is your job not just to administer a church program but actually to usher people into the throne room of God. Ultimately, it's an awesome privilege not to be taken lightly. I pray that God will bless the work of your hands and make you prosperous in every good work you do for His kingdom. Your reward will be great in heaven for what you've done on earth to bless those God loves.

Volume 2

Please do not forget to look out for volume two of this book. It focuses on the all-important areas of:

- How to develop your problem-solving skills

- Making leadership relevant

- How to create maximum impact

- Leadership traits to be avoided, etc. You do not want to miss it.

Personal Notes

_____

_____

_____

_____

_____

_____

_____

_____

BIBLIOGRAPHY

Biblical Principles of Leadership Succession and Development from Joshua 1:1-18

Life Application Study Bible (Tyndale)

Lecture Notes (DR Nigel Wright)

Management Information Systems (T Lucey)

21 Irrefutable Laws of Leadership (John C Maxwell)

The Maxwell Leadership Bible (John C. Maxwell) References:

Abrashoff, Captain D. Michael, *It's Your Ship: Management Techniques from the Best Damn Ship in the Navy*, New York, Business Plus (Hachette Book Group), 2002

Bennis, Warren, *Managing People is Like Herding Cats*, Provo, Utah, Executive Excellence Publishing, 1999

Blaber, Pete, *The Mission, The Men, and Me: Lessons from a former Delta Force Commander*, New York, Berkley Caliber, 2008

Johnson, Spencer, *Who Moved My Cheese?* New York, G. P. Putnam, 1998

Oakley, Ed, and Doug Krug, *Leadership Made Simple: Practical Solutions to Your Greatest Management Challenges,* Centennial, CO, Executive Leadership Solutions, 2006

Ray, Charles, *Things I Learned from My Grandmother about Leadership and Life,* Baltimore, MD, Publish America, 2008,

Taking Charge: Effective Leadership for the Twenty-first Century, Baltimore, MD, Publish America, 2009

Smith, Perry, *Rules & Tools for Leaders: A Down-to-Earth Guide to Effective Managing,* New York: Penguin Books, 1998

Related WSJ Articles and Blog Posts:

Firms Step Up Training for Front-Line Managers

Micromanagers Miss Bull's-Eye

Management Leaders Turn Attention to Followers

Companies Need CEOs to Stop Spinning and Start Thinking

Video: Steve Ballmer on How to Run Meetings

Video: BlackBerry Chief on Building Good Teams

Video: Steve Ballmer on How to Make Decisions

Strategic leadership institute

Anita Hall, Extension Educator Leverne Barrett, Extension Leadership Specialist University of Nebraska–Lincoln Index: Communities and Leadership Development Issued March 2007

Source: *Wisegeek -*

Marlene Chism is the author of Stop Workplace Drama (Wiley 2011). or at

www.christiangrowthnetwork,com/teachablespirit.html

The CFI Team

AUTOBIOGRAPHY

Glen Kerr is an ordained pastor and the founder of Pneuma Life Transformation Ministry Intl. A long-time qualified financial professional, he is a graduate of the London Guildhall University and the Brixton Bible Institute London, UK, respectively. Postgraduate in accountancy (Chartered Association of Certified Accountants) ACCA, Association of Accounting Technicians (MAAT), and an honorary MBA, BA (Honors) Degree, and Diploma in Higher Education. Glen Kerr has been a Christian for over 35 years and has served in numerous church positions. He has an evident apostolic anointing on his life, confirmed by word of knowledge/prophecy and a powerful demonstration. His ministry has taken him to several countries and continents worldwide, including Europe, The Caribbean, Africa, North America, and Asia, in an ongoing effort to empower the Body of Christ and win souls for the kingdom of God. He resides in the UK.

OTHER BOOKS BY THE AUTHOR

How to Effectively Share Your Faith With Confidence, Compassion and Understanding, Regardless of a Persons Background in Easy Steps

A STUDY GUIDE TO PERSONAL EVANGELISM

EMBRACING YOUR CHALLENGES

How Courage, Confidence, and Faith Transform Hardship Into Triumph and Success

www.ingramcontent.com/pod-product-compliance
Lightning Source LLC
Chambersburg PA
CBHW060948230426
43665CB00015B/2106